Soul
FARMER

Soul FARMER

SOWING SEEDS OF *change*

TO REAP AN INSPIRED LIFE

Dena Jansen

wordsmatter@cherrylooppublishing.com

ISBN: 978-1-7340713-5-1 (paperback)
ISBN: 978-1-7340713-6-8 (ebook)
ISBN: 978-1-7340713-7-5 (hardcover)
ISBN: 978-1-7340713-8-2 (audiobook)

Library of Congress Control Number: 2023921267

Printed in Buda, TX

Ordering Information:
Special discounts are available on quantity purchases by corporations, associations, and others. For details, contact author at getinspired@denajansen.com or visit denajansen.com.

Publisher's Cataloging-in-Publication Data

Names: Jansen, Dena, 1979- .
Title: Soul farmer: sowing seeds of change to reap an inspired life / Dena Jansen.
Description: Buda, TX : Cherry Loop Publishing, 2024. | Summary: Helps readers look at both the life they are currently living and the life they dream of experiencing, and provides tools to bridge any divide between the two, including a formula to help create a life in which change is embraced rather than run from.
Identifiers: LCCN 2023921267 | ISBN 9781734071375 (hardback) | ISBN 9781734071351 (pbk.) | ISBN 9781734071368 (ebook) | ISBN 9781734071382 (audiobook)
Subjects: LCSH: Change (Psychology – Handbooks, manuals, etc. | Self-actualization (Psychology) – Handbooks, manuals, etc. | Self-control. | Inspiration. | BISAC: SELF-HELP / Motivational & Inspirational. | SELF-HELP / Personal Growth / Happiness. | SELF-HELP / Emotions.
Classification: LCC BF637.C4 J46 2024 | DDC 158.1 J--dc23
LC record available at https://lccn.loc.gov/2023921267

For Mom and Dad –
This book is inspired by and for
the people you have been,
the people you are today, and
the people you have yet to become.

and for JP –
For choosing to grow alongside me.

TABLE OF CONTENTS

ABOUT ME

Hello, dear reader. It seems only right to share a little bit more about who I am so you can know my heart as you read all the words I have strung together in this book. I am a podcaster, women's event producer, and life coach who speaks to, gathers, and works with women who are ready to grow. They are smart, successful, business-owning, corporate-ladder-climbing, family-rearing, and relationship-driven creators. They are strong-willed women who somehow find themselves at a point in their lives where they no longer feel "like they used to." Often, they say they feel "lost" or "stuck." Many of them share a sense of fear or anxiety about a loss of forward momentum, but at the same time their mind is stuck in overdrive. Meanwhile, their spirit is waning.

Unlike some in that dilemma, however, they trust their gut enough to accept the work that's required and to seek out positive change. That's where I come in. I show up as best I can for women looking for inspiration, practical tools, and accountability to help them know that they are not alone when they make that coura-geous choice. The "why" behind my work is always to help guide them toward their next inspired steps. I remind them that they have options, they have free will, they have the power to make changes in their lives for the better. Those who hear me speak, or attend my events, or work with me quickly find out that my goal is for them to lean into curiosity as they ask themselves brave questions like, "What do I want?" or "What am I waiting for?" I help women dream again (or dream for the very first time). I help clients shine a light on all the options available to them, and I help hold them accountable for taking inspired action toward the longings of their heart. In a very real way, I share my heart so that other women can connect with their very own.

It is an absolute honor to serve women in that way and to gain the trust of someone looking for help in their life journey.

The truth is that I was my first client. I know what it's like to be in a season of life where you feel trapped rather than hopeful for what's to come. I shared my growth story in my first book, *Road to Hope: How One Woman Went from Doubting Her Path to Embracing Her Inner Journey*. Writing and publishing *Road to Hope* was a learning process and an absolute labor of love. In the pages of that book, in the stories that I shared, I found healing and ultimately, my truth—that the choice to prioritize the relationship I have with myself is the most beautiful, loving, and impactful decision I could ever make. I fell in love with myself and my commitment to be the Seeker I was born to be. By sharing my story in *Road to Hope*, I hope I have inspired other women just like me to hit the road toward their own hopes, dreams, and potential.

But I didn't stop growing after *Road to Hope*. Nope. I kept living and learning and further cemented for myself not only what it means to create an Inspired Life, but a process others could use to navigate and create their own. And I'm honored to present in this book, *Soul Farmer*, what I wish I'd had when I started my own personal growth journey. A book that offers more than just inspiration, but also new language and practices that I created over the ensuing years as I kept pursuing my Inspired Life that I'm confident will help others that are ready to grow.

Yet underlying all that creative, life-changing work through both books, I still hold my license as a Certified Public Accountant in the State of Texas. I retired from my public accounting career in 2018, leaving an amazing firm in Austin as a partner managing the nonprofit practice. Call it my need for a professional fallback (or the fact that I think CPA really means that I **C**ouldn't **P**ass that test **A**gain), but I keep that license in my back pocket. As a number-cruncher for many years and an auditor by trade, I was literally paid to be curious and ask good questions. I still find something beautiful in a solid equation or of things adding up nice and neat, and that's why it made sense to share the heart of this book in one simple, life-changing formula:

The Growth Cycle + YOU-Turns = An Inspired Life

I have chosen—*am choosing*, every single day—to be a Seeker. I am choosing to grow toward my Inspired Life. I make YOU-Turns, and I have lived through countless Growth Cycles.

Honestly, I've made too many choices in my life to count. But the choice that I am most proud of now is that I can honestly say that I am choosing to try. I am trying to create and experience my Inspired Life. I am choosing to live and learn—and more than that, I'm choosing to share whatever wisdom I have with people just like you who are ready to choose to try.

Please don't see me as an "expert" who works in a fancy office or teaches graduate students. I don't have a string of acronyms following my name. I'm just an everyday, homegrown, suburban woman who is trying to do her thing, sharing her life in the hopes that it inspires the next woman toward her own growth. I feel my life's work is to breathe light and life into the Seekers of the world. I wrote this book for you to pick up when you feel like you are settling for less than you deserve, when you find yourself stuck, or to gift a friend when you see them struggling with confidence and clarity as they try to find their next everyday brave steps forward toward more peace.

Moreover, I can't tell you how to solve your problems or fix your life in a few simple steps. I can't guarantee that everything will work out the way you'd like. There are too many things out of my—and yes, your—control.

But I can guarantee you this: You are capable of creating and experiencing your Inspired Life. I know you may not know how to do that yet, but that's why you are turning the pages of this book. You are longing to feel alive, awake, and enthusiastic (and yes, maybe a little nervous too) about making changes for a better life, and the only way to do that is to try something new. In the pages of *Soul Farmer*, I share new language and practical tools to help you do just that—learn and practice a new way to create your Inspired Life.

INTRODUCTION

A farmer dies when he stops farming, as the saying goes.

I learned that adage because I married a man who knew from the ripe old age of eight that he wanted to be a farmer. When we met at 15 years old, my high school sweetheart (and now my husband), JP, brought family farming into my world. I wasn't a complete newbie—both of us were born and raised central Texans—but back then, I thought of farming as fields, crops, tractors, maybe some chickens. I didn't know any *real* farmers. And I did not know how real farm life worked.

My husband is a real-life farmer. One who proudly farms with his dad on what some might consider a small family farm, but his love for farming is anything but small. Growing up with farms on both sides of his family, the seed for farming was planted at an early age, and that seed sprouted into a full-fledged, deeply rooted passion for growing things. As an adult, JP turned that seed into a career that he enjoys (mostly) every day.

He's grown corn and wheat, but his favorite crop is cotton because of its complexity and potential. "Cotton is a fickle plant," as he describes it. He knows that a cotton crop needs more care and attention as the growth season progresses. He likes the challenge of figuring out exactly what the cotton plants need to grow in any given season. He views the potential to produce and earn more as a challenge and risk worth taking, because if the markets are in his favor there could be a higher return on his investment. But over time, as he grew thousands of acres worth of crops, he also grew into a man who divided his time and attention as best he could between his farm fields and his family.

And where did I fit into all this farming business? Considering I am known for killing any plant that is left under my care, I was not the ideal candidate to join in his work. Add to that the fact that he fell in love with farming first, before he even met me. Knowing that I was his second love led to resentment in my heart for many years. So, I put quite a bit of distance between myself, the farm, and obviously then, my husband.

That approach did not serve us well. As much as I could logically understand his need to be away, to tend his fields, to plan, prepare, plant, maintain, and then harvest his crops to the benefit of our family, my feeling like less of a priority to my partner still stung my heart.

Then in 2015, in our 15th year of marriage while tending to our family with a son and daughter whom we love more than anything, our marriage neared a silent, devastating tipping point.

I was 36, a perfect age for a mid-life crisis. As it turns out, I was already thinking of one in terms of my career, where I was considering a professional transition. I was trying to decide whether I would actually walk away from a cushy corporate role as a partner at an amazing accounting firm. Did I want to leave that predictability behind in order to join the world of solopreneurship? Would it work for my family? What would I do all day? This decision was fraught with fear, too… fear of losing money, benefits, and financial security. It was not an easy decision for any couple to navigate, let alone one already struggling within their marriage.

My husband and I had been slowly becoming more and more apathetic about our relationship. It was, to use a farming term, undergoing a drought. Without the care and concern our marriage needed, cracks were appearing, and I wasn't sure we could fill them. I was feeling alone in my marriage and simultaneously feeling lost in my ability to make a decision about my next steps professionally.

I was longing for certainty and a balm to the chaos that I felt in my heart when another man came into my life and gave me just the attention I didn't know I needed. Before I knew it, I was wrapped up emotionally with a man who was not my husband.

So, in the fall of 2015, with a trembling heart and hands, I sat in our living room on the opposite side of the couch from my husband and had one of those talks that married people don't warn you about. The talks where your skin prickles and your palms sweat because for once in a marriage where everything usually feels routine and predictable, at that moment everything seems to be wildly up for discussion. Do we stay together or not? Do we sleep in the same bed tonight or not? Do we love each other or not? Are we committed to this marriage or not?

No one warns you about those talks, but they happen. They are scary as hell, and they hurt just the same. But they are also huge opportunities to get back on the same page and grow together, which, thankfully, is what my husband and I decided to do. We decided that we still had work to do together. And we decided that our marriage, and our love, was in fact a daily choice—one that we'd both have to make with each rising and setting sun.

I remember looking at my husband's tear-stained face and saying, "I can no longer guarantee that we're going to make it through this. But I am here today and still ready to try and figure it out."

After that conversation, I cut all ties to the man who was not my husband. As I did that, I was thankful that our emotional affair had never turned physical. I also made sincere apologies to myself and JP for the damage I had done. I'd broken my husband's heart and severely bruised the trust he had in me and us. Yet with our recommitted and shaky married legs under us, we started to venture through our next steps. Once the ground under our marriage settled a bit, we began to explore what it would look like for me to walk away from six figures and excellent benefits into a world of launching my own business—one based on inspiring other women through my own stories and lessons. I dreamed of myself under bright lights speaking to crowds of women, giving them the hope, the power, and the belief that they could make their own dreams become a reality. While how I'd actually do that was blurry, intention gave me the business name that I still use today: Dena Speaks.

A few months later, life threw us yet another curve ball when my mom decided to make the brave decision to seek a divorce from my dad. This wasn't easy for any of us, of course. My parents' marriage hadn't been one I would have put on a pedestal, but they were still my parents, and when you see two people you love hurt, you hurt. But the decision was made, and we had to deal with what came after.

And as I sat across the table from my dad one afternoon at a local Mexican restaurant with chips, salsa, and tacos on the way, we talked about the divorce. He was pretty quiet; I felt nothing short of awkward, but that seemed normal for the weird place in which we found ourselves. He didn't want the divorce, but he didn't have much of a choice since my mother wasn't offering options for reconciliation. Her decision was made. I knew he was hurting… that much was obvious. But he'd always kept his feelings to himself, so I had no practice being an emotional support to him. But even if I had, I wouldn't have been prepared for what came next. After taking a long drink of his iced tea, he served up to me something that I could barely swallow about his marriage—their marriage—something which I'd probably known in my heart but never imagined he'd say out loud. He said:

"I would have limped along until we died."

I felt like the wind had been knocked out of my gut. It was the opposite of anything I'd ever want to hear said about a relationship that I was a part of, let alone my parents'. Your parents are supposed to be your guides, your models for how to create all things good in the world. Yet his sentiment screamed nothing but dispassionate resignation to enduring life in an unhealthy and unfulfilling partnership. It scared me to think he could live that way, and in a sense, I was glad that he—or rather, my mom—had chosen not to. But sticking firmly to my childhood patterns, I said nothing in that moment. All I could do was scream silently in my head, "Well thank God she left. Who would want to live like that, limping along, dragging themselves through each day? Who would want to partner with someone like that? Who would endure waking up each day wishing for something, hoping for change, but expecting nothing but despair? "

At the same time, my heart broke for him. My dad was a recovering alcoholic of 30+ years. He'd done what I truly believe was the best he could every day to live one day at a time. He tried his best, and it wasn't enough to save their marriage. I felt so bad for him. I also acknowledged that my heart was breaking for my mom. She was a woman deeply mired in codependency who'd done her best to raise two daughters, work in and outside the home, and live one day at a time. Then, something changed: My mom reached a final tipping point and decided that despite the fact that she was a woman in her 60s who'd never lived an adult day on her own, she would rather face the unknown than remain in a marriage that was not alive and well.

What surprised me was that a part of me was jealous of her. Even though JP and I were standing firm by our decision to keep our marriage and family intact, I wanted to find the same level of courage and freedom my mother was venturing toward. How could I find my authentic best life? It sounded exciting, real, meaningful. But I could also see how it was scary. Scary to try something new. Scary to take risks. Scary to figure out how I could be my own woman, while actively working to rebuild my marriage, mother two children, and create a business that was nothing but a blurry dream. Scary to try and figure out how to grow with all the unknowns.

So, I spent some time—okay, actually lots of time—thinking about all of this. I mostly kept my thinking inside my own head, ruminating on the current realities of my marriage, my career, my life, but even more so about what the heck it was I really wanted. I wasn't entirely certain where I landed on it, but I did know two things for sure:

#1 – I did not want to limp along until I died. Not in my life, not in my marriage, and not in my work. It was time to make personal changes in my life, changes for the better, changes that would leave me feeling happier, healthier, and more whole. Changes that would benefit me and those I love, and

#2 – I did not want to grow alone. I wanted to see what I was capable of, but I also wanted my husband by my side. I had faith that we could figure out whatever life was going to bring us as we navigated change. I had shirts made that proudly boasted, "We Will Figure It Out" on the chest. We had no clue how we would figure it out. But agreeing to have faith and hope in our recommitted love was something new for us to try.

I wanted things to change. I wanted a better version of my life to begin. I wanted to feel excited about my work. I wanted to feel invested in my marriage. I wanted to live an Inspired Life—one where I felt awake, alive, with some semblance of control over my destiny.

My heart and soul were screaming, "Don't settle, Dena!"

And from that moment on, I didn't settle. Since then, I wake up every single day and try to grow. I've tried to create the Inspired Life I long for. I might have limped through a day or two, but as soon as I could, I got back at it. I might have taken two steps back but only after taking several forward in a new direction. I kept at it. Looking back, I know that I have made so much progress changing my old ways of choosing comfort over fear, of choosing silence over difficult conversation, of choosing the status quo over embracing the wild unknown.

I am a different woman than I was in 2015—and not just because I've aged. I've grown into a woman brave enough to leave corporate life and explore entrepreneurship. I've created a women's event in my community that serves several hundred women, bringing them the growth, connection, and joy that comes from a supportive community. I've coached other strong-willed women to their own *aha!* moments of self-reflection and soul awakenings. I've written and self-published a memoir chronicling the tumultuous time of my own personal and professional transitions. I've allowed myself the freedom to slow myself down enough to savor time as more of a stay-at-home mom than businesswoman. I've partnered with my husband to grow together and experience a marriage that we are both proud of. And I've lived and learned and grown through it all.

I'm different now, in that I feel a calm sense of peace knowing that I haven't settled. I didn't just give up on myself and the longings of my heart. I still don't have all the answers. I still can't guarantee success in my professional or personal ventures or relationships—no one can. I still experience emotional highs and lows. But I know that I will grow. And as I grow, I know that I have a partner who will figure things out with me while he continues to figure things out for himself as well. Together, we have promised each other to move toward our Inspired Lives.

A Farmer's View of the Growth Cycle

So, how do you grow personally? No one teaches us those steps, yet each of us struggles through it. When I began this book, I wanted to help my readers through their own Growth Cycles by sharing my experiences and what I have learned in my coaching community. But I was still feeling stumped by how to explain that process. Then, I looked over at my husband one night as he was shucking his dusty and dirt-covered clothes before showering off the day's work and realized: Here's an expert in growth right in front of me! His literal job is to make things grow! How can I take his knowledge of plants and farming to help me understand the Growth Cycle from people's personal perspective?

So, I swooped in right then and there to interview him. He's not a man of many words, but when it comes to farming, it's not hard to get him talking.

"I need you to walk me through a crop cycle," I blurted out and sat with my iPad ready to capture the responses.

He replied fairly quickly with, "From the farmer's perspective or the plant's?"

At that moment, I'm pretty sure my face scrunched up and my head exploded just like the dang emoji. Different perspectives on growth?! I hadn't considered the distinction before. Not even trying to hide my excitement and realization, I replied, "Umm, both please."

"Well, from the farmer's perspective it goes like this. First, you prep the ground for the seeds to grow. You plow, fertilize, and clear out weeds. Next, you plant the seeds. Then, after you've planted, you provide those seeds with all they need to grow. You do whatever it takes that is within your control to help the crop be the best that it can be. You are trying to maximize potential, remove obstacles and competition, and feed it whatever it needs to grow. We're dryland farmers, so I can't control when it rains. We have to do the best with what we get and control what we can control. Then when it's go-time, you harvest. You have to be able to gauge readiness, which is specific to each crop and environment. Then you sell it or store it with the goal always to maintain quality, impact others for the better, have low to no waste, and make money. Motive matters for the farmer. So, before every year, we sit down and do our best to plan out the year as well as to plan for a profitable operation."

His brief synopsis was the Growth Cycle from the perspective of the farmer—*my* farmer, rather. From my perspective as a farm wife, what JP said made a lot of sense because the farmer is a day-in-and-day-out *do-er*. Farmers trust in the repetitive patterns of nature, growth, life, and death. Their lives revolve around seasons, seemingly endless work to be done, fields to be cultivated, crops to be tended to, and equipment to purchase, maintain, and repair. They do the same thing over and over again—plant, grow, harvest—yet, every single day and season is different. There are so many external factors—water or lack thereof, too little or too much sun, insects, changing commodities markets, to name a few. Accounting for all of those issues in advance just isn't possible, yet they continue to farm.

My mind kept reeling with more things I'd witnessed of farming over the years. Farmers look for new tools to help them do what they do better. They want to improve their profitability and efficiency. But being a grower of things takes time. Traditionally, their work ethic borders on workaholism, but only because the work never seems to be done. Something always breaks. There's a new obstacle to conquer. And when one crop cycle ends, a new one must begin. There isn't time to focus on celebration. Crop production and commodity prices control the mood rather than persistence and passion.

Farmers are an endangered breed: Their circles of cherished community are dwindling, yet farmers need and understand each other. Together they share in the hard, uncomfortable reality of their passion. Farmers manage physical challenges right alongside the financial struggles of farming. They struggle under the emotional burden of trying to tend to their families as well as their farms. Some outsiders might assume they are simple-minded, but I'm here to say that people who dismiss farmers are missing the complexity of the farmer's chosen work. It's a "go, go, go get it done before the rain comes" way of living. It's about putting all you have into something with zero guarantees. Farmers farm. Their life's work is to grow many things from one seed. I felt I was finally understanding JP's work in a new way. And that's when our conversation took an unexpected turn.

I was feverishly typing notes when he continued, "But for the plant it's a bit easier, I guess." JP was about to lay out the Growth Cycle for me from a different perspective—that of the plant. Genius! During his summary of the farming Growth Cycle, I hadn't even let my mind consider how the plant endures, survives, and thrives. But of course, my farmer had! Here is what he told me:

"The seeds get stuck in the ground. They fight like heck to get out of the ground. Then they grow. Each type of plant just knows what it's supposed to do. But while each plant might turn out a little different, each is the same in that their life's work is to multiply. After seeds do their growth thing, though, they all eventually die at harvest time."

Here is where my mind kept slowly exploding and where I thought we maybe had a problem. I love JP to death, and his farmer skills and knowledge are so impressive. But, in my opinion, his comment that the seed's work is easier than the farmer's simply is not true. If we oversimplify the seed's life to being born, living, dying, we are missing the true beauty and wonder of growth. That tiny little seed has to work really, really hard to bust out of its casing, push both up and down through inches of heavy and hard dirt, in order to crack through the ground and feel the warmth of the sun while spreading roots to keep it grounded. We just don't give it much credit because we can't quite put into words the seed's experience. The dang thing can't talk to us. But somehow, the seed's experience still spoke to me.

My racing train of thought pumped the brakes as I had a realization.

What if the seed's life experience was similar to that of yours and mine? Of all of us? When it comes to humans—you and me—we too have a seed that was planted in us. One that we didn't really have any control over. And I believe that seed is our soul. Our soul—or what we might call our heart, our spirit, our essence—it longs to grow. It longs to have meaning and purpose. Somehow, our soul just knows that it's supposed to grow and multiply. All humans have a wildly active mind, a body full of thoughts and feelings, and a soul that is trying to talk to us.

But sometimes, it's hard to listen to what our soul is telling us. Short of religion for some or spiritual practices that others might consider too woo-woo, no one ever teaches us how to create an active, loving relationship with our soul so that we can help usher it through all the growth that it longs to have, all the impact it wants to make, and all the life it wants to experience!

In my mind, the problem is a two-fold question. First, how do we learn to listen to our soul? Second, with lack of training, how do we learn to prioritize intentional self-reflecting over mindless "doing?" Without language and tools in our growth toolkit to help us understand, we spin our wheels trying to move forward, but not truly growing. We end up feeling lost, alone, helpless, and hopeless when what we long for is growth, connection, and joy.

That night as we spoke, JP left me with one last thought:

"It's not easy work for the farmer or the plant," he said. "Everything changes on a dime. Rainfall comes and goes—too much water or droughts can make or break a season. Bugs come and go. Freezes or extreme heat make growth hard. Nothing is guaranteed. But that's how it works. And even though there are no guarantees, it's all still worth it to me."

Wait, did he just explain some basic truths of life that I was struggling to get down on paper?

Life isn't easy. Things are always changing. Change is an opportunity to grow. So much is out of our control. There are no guarantees. Life is effing hard. But an Inspired Life is absolutely worth showing up every single day ready to grow. That's just how it works. If you want to put down roots, push up stalks, face the sun and rain, and grow gorgeous green leaves and colorful blossoms, you have to work. Seeds know. Souls know.

Wow! Those insights were much more than I expected to get from that conversation with my husband.

I stared dumbfounded at my farmer-man and did my best to tell him how grateful I was for his quick rundown. I told him: "I think you just helped me figure out my book—why it matters, how it works, and what's missing for all us humans out there trying to live an Inspired Life." Then I gave him a big hug and ran to find my computer to flesh out such wonderful ideas.

All the Tools to Grow Are in You

Let me make clearer what this little interview cemented for me in my mind by one simple sentence: *Perspective matters.*

The farmer can't farm without the seed, and the seed can't grow without the farmer. And while I longed desperately to try and live an Inspired Life, there was a strange fact that I never understood before hearing my husband's words—**I am the farmer of my life, and I have a soul that I trust is the seed. Both the "thing" that needs to grow—my life—and the tools I need to grow it—my soul—are *within* me (or you!). Within all of us. What a revelation!**

Like most people, I was never taught how to grow, and I sure as heck was never taught that one of the biggest components of growth is perspective. Perspective is important because I need to be able to stand back and view my life as an observer, as a person with autonomy to make my own choices, with a mind and will to determine my next steps, and to analyze what I need to maximize my own potential.

I also need to trust that I have a soul with very real longings to grow, to have purpose and meaning, to feel alive and passionate, and to feel seen and heard as I live alongside other beautiful souls trying to do the same. I have to embrace and embody the hopes and dreams of the farmer *and* the hopes and dreams of the little seed too.

As the farmer of my life, I want to first create a vision and motive for my life to cement why I am here. What do I want? Then, I want to prepare my world for growth. I want to plant seeds of hope and of inspired action and give them all they need to grow. I want to control what I can control as I remove obstacles and maximize my potential.

At the same time, I have to fight to grow. I have to weather storms, feasts, famines, and a ton of unknowns to do what I think is right for me, to keep growing up and out while also putting down strong roots. Through all of those labors, I just keep growing and growing until it's time to harvest my fruit or prune things to allow for even better results. Then at some point, I have to know that like all living things, I will die. My time will come to an end, but with a sense of calm knowing that I tried day in and day out to grow. I need to know that I farmed my life and did it as best as I could.

To that end, I created a new mantra: Growth requires perspective. Growth requires consistent practice.

Saying both facts out loud is when I remembered the other truth that a farmer dies when he or she stops farming. If you take away the dirt, the seed, the long days and nights focused on caring for something and helping it grow—the farmer will die. Their heart might still beat, but their soul will fade, and they'll quickly find themselves limping through life.

And as I looked back at my life, I realized that I had stopped tending to my fields. My heart and soul were slowly dying because I didn't know how to nurture them.

I was stuck in a busy but unfulfilling state until I had what I call my soul awakening in 2015. After the crisis that nearly took out my marriage, and after I saw my mother making her own brave but scary choice to pursue what was most meaningful for her, I was sparked back into life with a drastic realization that I still had work to do on the farm that is my one, precious life. My mom reminded me that it's never too late to make a choice for yourself to grow toward what you really want. So, I did the work, day in and day out. And lo and behold, I grew because I figured out these essential practices to creating my Inspired Life:

- How to connect with myself and who I want to be.
- How to love myself with grace and generosity.
- How to commit to the pursuit of my potential.
- How to embrace curiosity over certainty.
- How to grow—and not just to age, but to evolve into a wiser, more fulfilled version of myself.

And an Inspired Life is what I want for you. I want you to show up for your one, precious life, ready to grow.

If you want that too but don't know what the hell it *means* to grow, let alone *how* to grow, I get it. I didn't either. But remember there is an equation from which we can and must learn, and the math is simple:

The Growth Cycle + YOU-Turns = An Inspired Life

Your Inspired Life Awaits

So, what exactly is an Inspired Life? Let me give you an example, an example I know really well, because it comes from the time that I spent writing this book. As I prepared to write #Book2in2022, as I so cutely hash-tagged it, I was *so* excited to get down to writing. In fact, I was so excited that I felt a bit uninspired by the other tasks I had on my monthly to-do list. I had social media posts to create and publish. I had a monthly email to my Dena Speaks community to write and send. Of course, those things are an important part of my profession. I enjoy doing these tasks every few weeks. But at that moment, I was really *inspired*, and I didn't want to miss out on that momentum.

So, instead of creating my Instagram content and writing my newsletter, I emailed the list of several hundred of my online friends and community members and told them I needed to get my inspiration onto the page. I said I'd be offline for a bit, busy with what was calling to me.

And I did what I said I would be doing. I wrote. It took longer than I wanted, and the journey wasn't as direct as I thought it would be, but I did it. After that, I felt inspired again—this time to reconnect with my email community and share that I sincerely appreciated their understanding of my need to take time off to write and focus my energies on other things that matter to me, then rest and recharge before returning.

That bit of my personal journey helps to explain one of the central concepts of this book: *to live an Inspired Life and what that means*. It means slowing down your busy days, focusing on what you really want to accomplish, and prioritizing self-care practices that bring you joy. Truly living an Inspired Life gives a bonus of restoring energy to return to life, your work, your family and relationships, renewed and reinvigorated.

With inspiration is how I want to live my life—with a sense of calm, focused, and ever-renewing energy even as I weather normal and natural waves of disruption and change. I want to feel like I have taken a deep breath of fresh air rather than gasping and grasping just to get through each day.

Instead of feeling stuck, listless, or "limping through life," I want to experience the constant and consistent, yet deeply personal and unique, Cycle of Growth with a spirit of humble curiosity.

Simply stated, I want to live an Inspired Life.

By that statement, I am committed to the pursuit of my potential—meaning I love and value exactly who I am, today, knowing that I have done the absolute best that I can with the knowledge, tools, and lived experience I have.

In my Inspired Life, I am powered by everyday bravery. I am focused on confronting the boundaries of my comfort zone in safe and small ways as well as bigger and more risky ones when I need to. I show up with a disciplined consistency, knowing that I must keep growing day in and day out or suffer the consequences of self-complacency.

In any Inspired Life, grace is required. And I'm not referring to grace in the context of any religious dynamic. Grace in this context is an essential undercurrent of nonjudgmental, self-kindness, self-gentleness, and self-forgiveness. I need to give myself grace because I can't always be perfect at living my Inspired Life. I need grace because I sometimes stray from mindsets that serve me or from practices that support me. Let's face it, I'm freaking human and am often quick to judge myself and compare my life to others. So, I treat myself with grace and gentleness and forgive myself when I need to. I surround myself with others who also focus on grace rather than judgment.

Likewise, pacing is paramount. Growth is a marathon, not a sprint. I'm here to grow for the long haul, so I trust myself and my body to tell me when it's time to speed up or slow down. I let time take time.

Last, I celebrate my own personal process and progress when appropriate (just like the farmer), and I do so with a sense of fun and anticipation. I try to stay in awe of myself and how far I've come, to appreciate all I've lived and learned, and to value what I still have to grow through.

But enough about *me*. Yes, my background is what anchors this book, but its purpose and goal is to help you create *Your Inspired Life*. I'm not a completely naive optimist, though, and I recognize that it is not easy work. I'm also pretty sure you're not looking for easy. In order to taste all the sweetness in the world, we need to remember sometimes what bitterness is. Sadness, disappointment, and fear are inevitable, and we all must face them. Yet when we focus on living an Inspired Life, we can tackle those challenges with less stress, less angst, and more peace. To do that, we continue to turn back toward the goal of living an Inspired Life.

When that determination gets challenging—as it inevitably will, sometimes—I'll show you how to use YOU-Turns repeatedly to help reconnect to yourself and find your next *inspired steps* forward. I emphasize *inspired steps* because I want any and all steps you take forward to be ones that you have thought about, that you are intentionally choosing, and that the next steps are on purpose for a purpose.

Then while keeping the vision of an Inspired Life in mind, you can use the YOU-Turns as a bedrock for growth and a means to weather each challenging Growth Cycle through which every Seeker's body, mind, and soul ventures. In choosing to grow, Seekers gradually release their grip on certainty and security and instead focus on curiosity. But they can and do trust in the ever-repeating Growth Cycle, which gives them a sense of peace in the process.

Seekers orient their lives around perspective and practice. They equip themselves with inspiration and practical tools. They celebrate progress. And they explore and find for themselves the best way to hold themselves accountable for the very thing they say they want: an Inspired Life!

Ultimately, the tool that every Seeker needs is the practice of self-reflection. That's why at the end of every chapter, you will find a Tool for Practice to help you slow down and give yourself, your heart, and your soul some well-deserved attention. Please don't discount the power of those Tools for Practice. While this book is full of so many of my words, the person you really need to learn to listen to is yourself. And you can't get better at that discipline unless you practice.

Since you are reading this book, you have a part of you that is ready to keep growing... a soul that is longing to be cared for... an Inspired Life that is begging to be lived. So, let's not waste another second. Let's dive into the first section—*Plant*—where we'll plant precious new seeds of hope, possibility, and growth, and start with perhaps the most important choice you'll have to make: *Will you choose to be a Seeker?*

Plant

Chapter 1
CHOOSE TO BE A SEEKER

The problem with growth is that it requires you to change. Or more clearly, it requires you to give into the fact that change is a required element of growth. But that's not all. After that acknowledgment, you must actively choose to *SEEK* growth through change!

The way I see it, the choice that life presents to all of us is this: *Will you choose to seek change as the agent for your very own beautiful and unique growth? Or will you view change as a vicious storm from which you hunker down and hide until it passes?*

You've picked up this book, so my gut tells me you are going to wholeheartedly—or, okay, maybe a little hesitantly—pick the former. You are choosing to embrace change as an agent for your life-giving growth because you are ready to create a renewed sense of excitement and enthusiasm for your life.

And for that, I *CELEBRATE* you with high fives, spirit fingers, and an off-beat booty shake!

It's a brave choice to make because the truth is you cannot change *and* stay the same. You are choosing to blossom and bloom into something new—fresh and full of new ways of thinking and being. You are choosing to be a Seeker!

What Is a Seeker

A Seeker is one who is attempting to find or obtain something. That explanation seems logical and is why the saying "seek and you shall find" makes sense. But let me break down the meaning and help take it from lower case *s* (seeker) to what I mean by a capital *S* (Seeker). To begin, notice that the definition of Seeker states that the person is attempting to find something. To seek never once guarantees that said individual will find what they are looking for, but they are *choosing to attempt to find* something. Or simply stated, they are *choosing to try.* That action puts a capital *S* on the word.

As a Seeker, you are choosing to believe that you must pursue growth because growth won't come from a standstill. Accordingly, you are choosing to accept that change is an opportunity to grow and is a necessary part of your personal evolution. You are choosing to trust that you will live and learn. You are choosing to believe that you can in fact figure "it" out (whatever "it" might be for you as well as whatever "it" is that life throws your way). You are choosing to show up time and time again to pursue your potential—the beautiful unknown between your current reality and what is possible for you and your life in the future—years, weeks, days, or hours from now. You are choosing to keep trying because you trust that you can't know unless you try.

Beyond improving your life, being a Seeker comes with other benefits.

- Seekers help create stronger families, friendships, businesses, and communities by choosing to grow themselves and by modeling to others what it looks like to choose to navigate personal growth and development through change.

- Seekers are a gift to the world because the positive changes they seek ripple out and impact others.

Among their other attributes, Seekers are driven, confident, scrappy, committed, curious, and crazy self-reflective. But Seekers are also apprehensive, cautious, critical thinkers, protective of themselves and others, and crazy HUMAN!

Seekers are not focused on perfection unless they're referring to the perfect night of sleep, cup of coffee, or slice of cake. Perfection is never the goal of a Seeker. Seekers focus on powerful and incremental change for the better for themselves and those they love. They choose to grow through and toward positive change.

Seekers also celebrate growth. They cheer on themselves and other Seekers for every meaningful baby step forward. They don't wait for "winning" results since those are never guaranteed—and who can define what a real "win" is for anyone else anyway? Rather, they celebrate the learning and growth throughout the process. They give themselves and others a high five in moments of happiness and joy just as much as they stand with others in moments of heartbreak and disappointment. They choose to trust that in all of the feelings that life evokes, there is learning and growth.

If you choose to become the Seeker that you were born to be, you devote yourself to seeking change for the better in your life. It's a bold choice, because I guarantee that in a matter of days, weeks, months, or years, you will not be the same person you are today. You, your heart, your soul, your mind, your perspective, your experience... all of it will shift and evolve with any change you make, and that is not only okay, it's fantastic!

As you explore throughout the pages of this book, you'll find that this way of living and being—*seeking growth through change*—will be the ultimate act of self-devotion. Read that again—it is an amazing act of self-devotion to choose to seek the change you want and need. Choosing this brave way of growing is not selfish. It is the most beautiful choice you can make for yourself and anyone else you share life with.

Choosing to embrace the Seeker's mindset affords you the opportunity to joyously create your Inspired Life! That's why I encourage (dare I say, implore) you to choose to be the Seeker that I know you can be.

Seekers Make Choices

Choosing to try is the heart of what it means to be a Seeker with a capital *S*. When you adopt the Seeker mindset, you are choosing to lead yourself to your Inspired Life. But when you choose to try, you are also choosing several other things for yourself. You are choosing to believe that you are meant to grow. You are also choosing to believe that without growth, your heart and soul will wither, and you will not experience the full, bountiful experience that life has to offer.

When you choose to be a Seeker with a capital *S*, you also choose to seek first the longings of *your* heart and soul. You choose to make a central part of your life all the needed YOU-Turns (which you'll learn more about in Chapter 4).

As a Seeker:

- You choose to regard yourself with the highest and utmost love and respect.

- You choose to prioritize yourself, trusting that by doing so you are not harming or diminishing the needs of others in your life (like family, friends, your business, your career, etc.).
- You choose to seek first to create a lasting relationship with yourself that is grounded in care and trust.
- You focus on your own emotional health. You choose to focus on staying safe amid chaos and emotional turbulence throughout your growth journey until your dying day, knowing you can only control what you can control.

Seekers choose to not get sucked into comparison. Seekers trust that their life is precious and unique, so it couldn't possibly look like anyone else's. They trust that no one Seeker's journey is the same. Seekers are attracted to other Seekers who choose to try and find whatever their heart and soul might be longing for—peace, adventure, belonging, love, joy, impact, the list could go on.

Being a Seeker is a life-changing choice—indeed, a lifestyle. I say lifestyle because it truly is a way of living that requires a certain mindset rooted in foundational attitudes that will guide you through the peaks and valleys of growth.

What It Takes to Show Up as a Seeker

If you want to experience steady and consistent growth as a Seeker, you must show up with three life-changing values planted deeply and rooted firmly in your heart: (1) humble curiosity, (2) everyday bravery, and (3) disciplined consistency. Now let's talk a little about how each of them works.

#1 - HUMBLE CURIOSITY

Humble curiosity is based on the idea that you don't (and can't) know all there is to know. That's why you must embrace the gift of humble curiosity. Don't allow your ego to stunt your growth by being too proud to embrace all that you don't know (and sometimes you don't even know what you don't know yet). Instead, take life as something to be explored, not dominated. Be open to the lessons the world brings to you.

Humble curiosity is about looking at each day as an opportunity to learn something new. Humble curiosity means getting really good at asking all the questions. It means opening your mind to seeing new ways of doing and being. Humble curiosity means that you realize you can't possibly know something unless you personally try. As a Seeker, you allow humble curiosity to remind you that what someone else says is true for them is not necessarily true for you. You embrace experimenting for yourself as a way to live and learn.

A Seeker's curiosity will develop and become more natural through time and experience. You have to practice being curious. Practice dipping your toe into something new—for example, raising your hand, sending an email to ask or answer a question, starting a blog, creating a piece of art—almost anything that you usually resist. Trust that your curiosities matter and are worth your time as they will guide you to growth.

A Seeker's humility will also increase and become easier to swallow with time and experience. You will shift from being fearful of not being the smartest in a room to embracing that there are always crazy smart people to learn from. Sometimes, you might fall prey to competitiveness and the need to "succeed" or "win" as you dive whole- (or half-) heartedly into something new, but with genuine humble curiosity leading the way, you'll find that there are no wins or losses—you are solely focused on learning. And I promise, you will learn something new every single time—and that is *always* a win.

Humble curiosity not only gives you the opportunity to seek and find new answers, it gives you the chance to grant yourself and others grace as you grow. Because the truth is this: Not one person has life figured out completely. No one has all the answers. So, give yourself a break, give other people a break, go figure out a little bit more about whatever it is you don't know yet, and try to have a blast stepping just outside your comfort zone and feeling the thrill of exploring the unknown.

WHAT DOES HUMBLE CURIOSITY LOOK LIKE IN REAL LIFE (OR IRL, LIKE THE KIDS SAY)?

- Submitting an online inquiry for more information on a program (e.g., self-defense class, college course, certification program of anything to which you are drawn, yoga, life coaching, etc.), or any variety of X, Y, Z online courses where you'll learn "how to" do something you are interested in. Then, if the curiosity persists, register and go to that activity, approaching it with an open mind.
- Texting a friend that you respect and admire to ask them how they juggle their personal and professional ambitions so seemingly well.
- Asking for candid feedback from your teammates, managers, and/ or clients in the professional setting *or* from your children, spouse/ partner, and/or friends, then genuinely using that feedback as an opportunity to improve.

> ✐ Reading (or listening to—thank you, Audible) a new book, listening to a new podcast, or watching a new documentary on a topic that piques your interest.

#2 - EVERYDAY BRAVERY

Fortunately for most of us, growth isn't a life-and-death situation. Instead, we are working to change our careers, to improve our relationships, to do more of what we like, or to live healthier lifestyles. These kinds of growth require plenty of change, but let's keep it in perspective: So many of us in the U.S. are privileged to live in safe environments for growth. For most of us looking to plant new seeds of hope for our lives, heroics will not be required, but I'm here to tell you that everyday bravery will be mandatory.

Changing your well-worn habits and patterns of behavior to try and grow will sometimes feel like you are stuck in foot-deep ruts that you can't possibly escape. But you can—and you will—if you truly want to show up and earn that capital *S* status. You'll do that by getting more and more comfortable being slightly uncomfortable. The truth of lasting and sustained growth is that it's often not made up of drastic measures, but instead built on the tiniest incremental pivots in your ways of thinking, doing, and being.

The question to ask yourself when looking for the next step in your everyday bravery is this: What is the smallest, safest, yet newest (to me) thing I can try? You don't have to make huge leaps of faith; you simply need to take small, inspired steps forward.

By showing up and choosing baby steps every day, you'll build your confidence. You'll have to allow yourself to experience the emotional journey that choosing everyday bravery brings into your world—which will include some serious highs and lows. But over time, you'll find that you will get better and better at conquering big fears with seemingly small, brave choices. Your heart might race a little less, your palms might not sweat as much, you'll get more comfortable being the Seeker you are choosing to be. You'll build a steadfast belief that in fact you are brave, bold, capable, and ready to grow.

WHAT DOES EVERYDAY BRAVERY LOOK LIKE IRL?

- Raising your hand at a meeting to ask a question when not one other person has said a peep.
- Picking up the phone and calling a friend or colleague to begin a difficult conversation that you know needs to happen.
- Offering a suggestion for improvement in some day-to-day process you go through with your family, at your office, or with a client with no expectation other than to start an open dialogue.
- Joining a new group in your personal or professional communities when you don't know anyone else there or are not sure if you have anything to offer.
- Saying no to a new opportunity or leaving a group that no longer serves you.

#3 - DISCIPLINED CONSISTENCY

You can't show up once and expect your world to change forever. As a Seeker, you must choose to *pursue* growth forever (yes, forev-va, evva, thank you '90s music). That means seeking opportunities to live and learn over and over again. And by trying new things with a steadfast consistency, you choose to believe that you can in fact figure "it" out. You keep trying because you trust that you can't know unless you try.

Disciplined consistency simply means that you believe in your core that you must KEEP GROWING! Growth is a long game, not a sprint. So, you'll choose to show up with disciplined consistency every new day in the way that feels right to you on that day. Some days you'll be kicking up dust with your focus and determination. Other days, you'll be on your hands and knees feeling like you are pulling out one stinking weed at a time. You'll redefine productivity as progress. You'll work hard, play hard, and when the time is right, you'll nap hard.

Just like on the farm, there will be seasons that have their specific time and purpose. As a Seeker you'll relish seasons that feel like spring, fresh and full of new growth and exciting new opportunities. But you'll also weather seasons that feel like a sweltering Texas summer, where you feel like you are battered, run ragged, and doing your best to not wither away. Those stages are where disciplined consistency comes in because as a Seeker, you learn to trust that every season serves its purpose.

The biggest threat to a Seeker is complacency. But disciplined consistency is your answer when you want to give into unhealthy patterns, old ways of being and doing that don't serve you, or when you simply feel tired of growing. You'll layer in rest and reflection and then get back on your trusted (and chosen) path of growth.

WHAT DOES DISCIPLINED CONSISTENCY LOOK LIKE IRL?

- Establishing routines and rituals that nourish your heart and soul, knowing that they can and most likely will evolve over time.
- Playing with different intensities when it comes to your life pacing, trusting you'll learn through time and experience when to pump the breaks or rev up your engine.
- Asking for and taking a sabbatical from work, a break from a committee, or any other step back from a responsibility you have to allow your mind to rest and gain clarity.
- Taking a solo-vacation to any place that fits your style and budget to give yourself space to just be where you want to be, do what you want to, and to recharge your batteries.
- Waking up every morning and choosing to show up ready to grow as best as you can on that new day!

Seekers are able to live in "the then, the now, *and* the what's next." They trust and respect their own journey and are ultimately in the pursuit of peace. Peace knowing that they have tried. Peace knowing they tried to show up well for themselves and those they care about. Through humble curiosity they own their mistakes and shortfalls, but also embrace those as opportunities to grow. Through everyday bravery, they prove to themselves that they are bold and brave and capable of trying and learning new things. Through disciplined consistency, they commit at a cellular level to showing up as the Seeker they were born to be and pursuing their potential as they create their Inspired Life.

Seekers choose not to see themselves as victims of life; rather, they see themselves as the creative writers of their own story, the farmers of their own fields. And armed with those hope-fueled attitudes they see the Growth Cycle as their ever-present, ever-evolving way to keep growing.

I believe you are ready to live a life full of self-directed change toward healthier, better-equipped physical, spiritual, mental, and emotional growth. But the choice will always be up to you. Will you choose the Seeker lifestyle, embrace the Seeker's mindset, and show up ready to grow?

Seek and You Shall Find

Throughout my work as a life coach and in time spent mentoring aspiring professionals, I have worked with women and men who have made changes for the better in their lives. Each had their own unique hopes and dreams for their growth. Each one had their unique set of life circumstances. Each one experienced their own growth in their own time. My clients, ranging in age from their 20s to 70s, confirm for me that growth is necessary and glorious at *any* age.

But even though they all are uniquely different, they all share one thing—a longing for clarity and a desire to live a more fulfilled life. They want to know what to do next. They want to know how to achieve whatever goal they came to the table with. They want to know how to feel inspired, passionate, excited about their life. They want to know the path forward.

Unfortunately, I cannot answer that for them—no one can, other than themselves. But I *can* help them start practicing at gaining their own clarity and expressing themselves as best they can.

That's why before every introductory session, I send them an email or text with ONE question:

What would need to happen for our time
together to be a WIN for you?

The reason I ask that question is that before we can work together to help them find their path forward, they need to ask themselves—and answer as best they can—the "what do I want?" question.

No one person has the same response because no one Seeker is the same. But here are some examples of what clients have told me would need to happen for our time together to be a win:

"Just being here and giving myself this time is a win."

"I'd want a plan, maybe not a comprehensive one, but at least the next few things I can try to move forward and stop being stuck."

"I'd need to feel like you've helped me identify options."

"I want to figure out what my 'it' is and how I can start to feel like myself again."

"I'd need ideas to help me have more confidence when it comes to making changes I know I'll need to make."

"I want help prioritizing my time into things I really love and enjoy rather than just being busy all the time."

To me, all of those answers share a common thread: People need time and space to find the confidence and clarity they say they want.

As a Seeker, there is a desire to have as much clarity as we can so we don't go out and live aimlessly, spreading ourselves thin like a vine or weed. But all too many times, we look for those answers in the wrong place. We look to our partners, our friends, our work, or society around us. But we don't stop to ask *ourselves* important clarifying questions.

It is that time in self-reflection—where we ask ourselves and clarify where we are, where we have been, and where we want to go—that reveals our true desires. The answers create what I call a Seeker Statement, a simple fill-in-the-blank sentence to help them define as best they can right now what they want, why they want it, and what positive change or impact it will bring to their life.

Putting what you want into a Seeker Statement, knowing that the outcome can and will happen over time, is an important first step for a Seeker.

My Seeker Statement right now might look like this:

I want to write and share the message of this book because it will help others get unstuck and create their Inspired Lives (which is freaking fantastic)!

But this book is not about me—it's about you!

So, here is your first Tool for Practice, where you have the opportunity to put what we just learned together into practice. My gut tells me you are gearing up to be the Seeker you were born to be, so let's practice putting words to your wants in your very own Seeker Statement.

Tool for Practice

CREATING THE SEEKER STATEMENT

Checking in with yourself to gain clarity is the goal, so there are actually two steps to creating your Seeker Statement.

Step 1: Devote time to self-reflection. Seekers learn to give themselves time and attention to think and reflect. For you this might be five minutes or five hours. During this time, let your mind clear and concentrate on your vision for your best life. What will truly make you happy, fulfilled, and content? What will make you want to jump out of bed in the morning and get your day started right away?

Step 2: Honestly express yourself. Here is where the writing comes in. A Seeker Statement is a simple fill-in-the-blank sentence to help you define as best you can what you want and why you want it—namely, what positive change or impact will it bring to your life? Seeker Statements can change over time (just like you!), and you might have multiple Seeker Statements swirling around in your mind at once. Don't let that derail you. Try not to focus on getting the Seeker Statement "right" because, well, there is no wrong way. The goal is to simply get something written down about what you think you want and why.

Go ahead and take your first stab at expressing yourself and your growth goals:

Seeker Statement: I want to _____

because it will _____.

Here's another way you might practice with a Seeker Statement. You could create a Seeker Statement focused solely on what your goal is by giving your precious and limited time and energy to this book.

Ask yourself: *What would need to happen for our time together through the pages of this book to be a WIN for you?*

Think about it: *Why did you pick up this book? What do you want to get out of it? What positive change might you experience in your life if you stick with me until the last page?*

Now, try and create a narrower Seeker Statement, related only to your commitment to reading and engaging with *Soul Farmer* cover to cover.

Seeker Statement: I want to _____
because it will _____.

To get in a better habit of asking yourself what you want and honoring your answers, maybe print out your Seeker Statement or grab a piece of paper, jot it down, and stick it somewhere you'll see it often. And even though your Seeker Statement will change over time, and even over the course of reading this book, the practice of verbalizing what you want and why is a steadfast tool that will serve you as you keep growing.

And now that you know why it's vital to choose to be a Seeker and are armed with a Seeker Statement, let's keep planting seeds that will one day bloom by learning how to *dream up your Inspired Life.*

Chapter 2
DREAM UP YOUR INSPIRED LIFE

Just as a farmer farms, a Seeker seeks. And even though, as the saying goes, assuming can make an ass out of you and me, I am going to continue operating under the hopeful assumption that you did in fact choose to identify as the Seeker you were born to be. You've got your Seeker Statement posted loud and proud in a place that will remind you of what you want and why. Keep it close by; it will center you in this growth journey.

Now, it's time to dive into the right side of the equation, the goal and sum of all the growth to come, an Inspired Life:

The Growth Cycle + *YOU-Turns* = ***An Inspired Life***

To support you as a Seeker, our first priority is to bring into better view the goals you have for your growth and help you create an *inspired* vision for your life. It's time to learn how to dream up your *Inspired Life*—one where you feel alive, awake, and with some semblance of control over your destiny. See the Seeker Statement as the path to travel to the Inspired Life, which is the goal.

What Is an Inspired Life

An Inspired Life consists of anything your heart desires *the most*. The formula to attain an Inspired Life is taking the action to achieve those desires.

So, how do you start? Figuring out what your desires are might seem simple at first, but sometimes we get stuck in imagining what will truly make us fulfilled and alive. True, being able to imagine your best life is so absolutely essential to human growth and happiness, but most of us limit our imagination to mediocre musings. The Inspired Life requires vision of your best life, the deep-down dream that you might often think about but have yet to act upon. Let me share some examples:

- My Inspired Life includes staying fairly close to home, continuing to learn about people and relationships (meaning lots of books and podcasts), creating memories with my family and friends, and inspiring myself and others. I want to trust, live, and learn alongside kind, open, and real people and to know that I have somehow positively impacted another human being on their life's journey. I want to live my life feeling full of inspiration—with a sense of calm and focus, thereby receiving ever-renewing energy even as I weather normal and natural waves of emotion, disruption, and change. I want to feel like I have taken a deep breath of fresh air rather than gasping and grasping just to get through each day.

- For one of my coaching clients, her Inspired Life requires travel and adventure. She simply cannot imagine a life that excites her without visiting foreign countries. She craves the adventure and experiences of traveling abroad. She loves seeing how people live in other countries, seeing how her life may be the same or how it differs. She loves to share her passion with other travel-lovers in an online community she created. She's even started taking others on tours. She connects to herself and others by making her worldview bigger.

- My mom's Inspired Life must include dancing. That's right, nearing her 70s, my mom lives to throw on her boots and dance her little heart out. And for far too many years, she watched the dance floor from the side, so now she is making up for lost time. The dancing, the music, and the people bring a rhythm to her life that fill her with joy and energy. Her Inspired Life also wouldn't be complete without her sisters, her daughters, her grandkids, and her Al-Anon community.

- My husband JP's Inspired Life includes dreams of driving his tractors back and forth for hours on end. (I'm not kidding!) He dreams of acquiring and adding more acres to Jansen Family Farms. He longs to work incredibly hard and to keep building a farm operation in which he has immense pride, and even more, one that others respect (and maybe even envy). He wants a farm shed that is big and beautiful and stocked with all the tools he needs to make fixing broken stuff easier. He wants to have his family close, safe, healthy, and happy. He wants to travel to a small handful of his favorite cities and visit his favorite restaurants.

As you can see, each of those four Inspired Lives looks completely different, and that's the point. We're not judging anyone else's dreams; instead, we're here to help uplift all of us toward what will bring us authentic joy and fulfillment. The thing about dreaming up an Inspired Life is that it is a very personal exercise with a very personal and unique result. An Inspired Life is all about finding what brings *you* joy, leaves *you* feeling spent but in a really good way, and is something *you* want even if it requires sacrifice or effort. Perhaps most importantly, an Inspired Life *gives* you energy rather than sucking it out of you.

So, take a deep breath right now and jot down what comes to mind when you think of your Inspired Life. What do you think you truly and deeply want? What would energize you and bring you joy?

In staring at a blank piece of paper, you might have no freaking clue how to answer either of those questions. You are not alone in feeling lost. I've had several women look me in the eye with a load of angst saying, "I have no idea what I want."

But trust me: You are not lost. You are here, ready to learn how to keep growing. So, rest easy… there are no right or wrong answers here. Keep in mind that your answer today is not written in stone. It can and will change over time. Give yourself freedom to jot down whatever comes to mind, even a laundry list of ideas that right now seem worthy possibilities.

In my Inspired Life...

Find Focus and Flexibility in Your Inspired Life

As you start fleshing out the details of how your own Inspired Life might look, remember this: Seekers trust that *The Growth Cycle + YOU-Turns = An Inspired Life.*

Seekers define for themselves what an Inspired Life means to them which allows for great flexibility, and that can be scary to some.

I have a few questions that always help guide my coaching clients—and me—toward the longings of our heart.

The first question is the one I asked earlier and is required because the answer will help you figure out your dream, your vision for your Inspired Life.

What do you want?

But don't fret: The answer is not only retractable but will change over time. Even if what you want might seem silly, simple, or ridiculously hard and out of reach, that's okay. What you want might even seem so far from what you are experiencing right now *or* maybe it looks almost exactly like the life you're living now. Either is fine. What we're really aiming for here is you getting more and more comfortable expressing that you do in fact have hopes and dreams and things that YOU *want.* Because, like everyone, you want things for your life! It's imperative that you believe that your wants matter, and it's your job to give them voice. Don't let your desires hide in the dark recesses of your mind where they will never see the light of day. Shine a light on them so we can work to bring them to life!

While keeping in mind that there are no right or wrong

answers to the question, there definitely is a wrong (yet very normal) way to think about your answers. The wrong (and much less productive) way would be when self-doubt and social comparison sneak in and ruin your progress—any of those things that keep you from your Inspired Life. That interference might show up after you first articulate what you want. Watch out if your very next thought is something like:

- *I could never do that.*
- *I don't have the money for that.*
- *I am not smart enough to accomplish that.*
- *Isn't someone else already doing that?*
- *But that isn't as big or fancy or prestigious as what human x, y, or z does or has?*

Such questions aren't helpful, which I know you know. Try to quiet their noise and focus on YOU. Instead of dwelling on the doubts and the negatives, ask yourself a follow-up question: *What is enough for me?*

That question can help you stave off comparison, because it helps put the focus back on you and no one else by allowing you to personalize and right-size your dreams. The question can be all about a specific thing, like your finances and material belongings (e.g., a two-bedroom apartment with great parking is enough for me, a salary that covers my living expenses plus two family vacations is enough for me). Or the question can help you focus on the values you will cling to like honesty, authenticity, abundance, compassion, and grace, and similar considerations that really matter to *you* (e.g., family, community service, entrepreneurship, wealth creation, travel).

The trick is this: If you can define what is enough FOR YOU, then you can let go of whatever big, big plans someone else has for themselves and stop comparing yourself to them. The point is to make *your* dreams become *your* reality. And I'm going to give you the opportunity to practice defining those things for yourself in this chapter's Tool for Practice.

Whether you are a stay-at-home parent or caregiver, corporate C-suite or new hire, business owner or community activist, you can give yourself time to answer for yourself (and maybe along with your partner/spouse/significant other) what is enough for you. But here's the biggest part of this quest—it will evolve over time. It will evolve as you learn how to make YOU-Turns and navigate the Growth Cycle. What is enough for you will become clearer and clearer, the more you show up ready to grow.

Dreams are not a "one size fits all." You have the freedom to choose the dream that feels right for you, knowing that size does matter—not for comparison's sake—but for the sake of honoring your heart and soul.

And regardless of the size of your dream, every Seeker makes progress the exact same way—by making choice after choice to show up with those three fundamental values of humble curiosity, everyday bravery, and disciplined consistency to keep growing!

As a Seeker, the real practice to build is getting more comfortable getting curious with yourself. So, close your eyes and ask yourself these questions out loud (yes, practice saying them with your actual voice):

What do I want?
What is enough for me?

Let answers bubble up and gently push aside any judgment that might pop up. Jot down your vision and what you hear in your inner self, and allow yourself grace if you get swept up into comparison. Don't forget to recenter your focus on *you* as often as necessary. The more you practice, the better you'll get at dreaming, wishing, hoping, and creating a vision about what you want, what is enough for you, and ultimately, your Inspired Life.

So, here is your next Tool for Practice: Practice dreaming. And while I want you to keep exploring the questions we've already covered, this is a particular exercise designed to help you dream up a perfect day. In imagining your perfect day, you will be giving yourself clues about how your Inspired Life might look. By giving yourself space to dream, you narrow down for yourself what really matters to you and should be part of your Inspired Life. Remember, have fun with this! And don't censor yourself—it's a-okay to set reality aside for a bit and create a newer, more exciting, more fulfilling vision for your Inspired Life!

Tool for Practice

DREAM DAY EXERCISE

Grab a cup of coffee or your beverage of choice, a pen or pencil, and something to write on. Get comfy and ease into what I like to call the Dream Day Exercise. This is normally a guided process that I walk clients through, but you can do it all on your own—or have a friend or spouse/partner help you through if you want to play with someone.

The Dream Day Exercise is pretty simple. You imagine that you wake up one morning in the future—at least one year from now, but maybe three or five years out—and you somehow know you are living the dream—your dream. Then I want you to write out how you feel, where you are, what you do, from the moment you open your eyes to the moment you rest your head back on your pillow at night.

Note the time, where you are, what you eat, what you're spending your time on, and who is there with you. Try to dispel judgment; just jot down what comes to your mind.

Allow yourself to continue to dream. Keep asking yourself, *what would I do next on my Dream Day?* If you get stuck, ask yourself, *what would I for sure NOT be doing on my Dream Day?* That is also valuable information.

Questions I like to include are how do you feel when you wake up (e.g., refreshed, peaceful, hopeful, etc.) and how do you feel when you end your day (e.g., rested, fulfilled, like you've contributed, spent, etc.)? It's always good to identify the way you want to feel and the energy that you dream is present.

Depending on why you picked up *Soul Farmer*, you could also personalize your Dream Day Exercise to address specific concerns you have. For example, if you find yourself in a professional plateau, then maybe specify for yourself that this is a Dream *Work*day, and spend your time focusing more energy on what you are doing, who you are working with, what the culture feels like, what impact you are making, etc.

When you're done dreaming up your Dream Day, the next step is to walk yourself (or your Dream Day buddy) back through your Dream Day. And I mean start from the top: *I woke up at __ a.m. feeling well rested and excited for the day.* And finish with: *I went to bed at ___ p.m., feeling _____.* I highly encourage you to read your Dream Day back to yourself out loud. There is power in hearing the dream come to life.

Then, pause… let the details settle in. Many of my clients experience different emotions as they listen to their Dream Days. That's normal. It's exciting to dream. It can also be scary. And it can for sure be informative.

After you've relished in your Dream Day, ask yourself this final question: *Is anything missing?* Seems like an odd question, but just ask, stay curious, and see if anything bubbles up. If not, cool. If yes, jot it down. Then sit back and give yourself a few more minutes to reflect on the exercise and how it might inform you about what you long for in your Inspired Life. Ask yourself questions like:

* What am I most excited about in my Dream Day?

* Do I see any patterns or themes of what really matters to me that might help me continue to craft and define my Inspired Life?

* Did anything in my Dream Day surprise me?

Then once you finish this Tool for Practice, I encourage you to let it go. And I don't mean forget about it. In fact, many of my clients keep their Dream Day notes close as a reminder of what's possible. What I mean by let it go is don't overthink it or get panicky about making it become your reality today. The Dream Day is not supposed to stress you out! Instead, just write it out and keep it close because we'll come back to it in Chapter 5.

We are still planting precious new seeds of a Seeker's identity, mindset, and vision. In the *Grow* section of the book we will learn how to make our dreams grow. But for now, I simply want you to keep expressing what you want as best you can, keep looking at your Seeker Statement, changing it as it feels right to you, and imagining that you live in that Dream Day of yours as you create your Inspired Life.

But I can't move on any further without tackling this truth—*there will be obstacles to growth.* That's why I invite you to turn the page and learn how to manage those growing pains. Keep reading so that you can keep growing.

Chapter 3

MANAGING GROWING PAINS

I asked my husband about how he deals with all the unknowns that the farming industry and lifestyle has to offer. He pondered for a second and took a deep breath before sharing, "All I can do is try to control what I can control and remove as many obstacles to growth as possible. I can do everything right and still not achieve the crop of my dreams. That's the risk I take when I farm. But I choose to keep showing up and trying because it's just part of the process—dealing with things that try to get in the way of growth."

My husband is not a man of many words, but those words came straight from his heart. He's also not known for being an endless optimist, like me. He's a pretty cut-and-dry kind of guy— just tells it like he sees it. I, on the other hand, bring the light and glass-half-full perspective to our relationship. That's why I'd rather focus on all the amazing aspects of growth. But it's important for us all to acknowledge that growth is not always easy, and it doesn't always turn out the way we want it to. This isn't only true for his farm operation—it's true for all of us (even me!).

Just like my farmer-man, Seekers like us can do everything right—we can show up with humble curiosity, with everyday bravery, and with disciplined consistency, with a Seeker Statement, and a unique vision for our Inspired Life—and still not reach all that we dream of. I'm here to remind you that we can and will experience our Inspired Lives, but not without struggles along the way. Because as JP says, there will always be obstacles that get in the way of your growth. The question is, how do you overcome them?

To start, you need commitment. Are you committed to keep growing? I hear you saying, *YES!* and I'm pumped for you, you Seeker, you. It's that kind of spirit that's going to carry you through and help you manage growing pains. And speaking of growing pains, let's just rip the bandage off and dive into what they are, how you can manage them, and give you some tools to help you build yourself up!

Keep an Eye Out for Obstacles to Growth

For JP, and farming operations all over the world, obstacles to growth include weeds, water (too much or not enough), nutrients that determine soil health, little on-plant pests, bigger land-roaming critters, and land erosion, just to name a few. There are also competing farms, labor shortages, and lack of resources or expertise that make farm life difficult. These obstacles can invade aggressively or slowly creep in and undermine the farmer's ability to farm or the seeds' ability to grow.

It's no different for a Seeker who dares to dream up and begin to create their Inspired Life. Obstacles will present themselves— sometimes slowly or other times quickly and without warning. But the Seeker's first step to manage any resulting growing pains is to acknowledge that the obstacle is present. Seekers don't ignore reality, and the reality is that change for the better won't always come easily or without challenge. Seekers assess risks to their growth, arm themselves with awareness, and layer in grace as they navigate difficulties.

Let's go over the top six obstacles that show up and make it hard for you to grow:

#1 -*Missing Nutrients* – Just like nutrients for the soil, your soul needs nutrients to grow. We all need nourishment, contribution, love and connection, significance, certainty, and even some uncertainty (or let's be real, life would get boring). We also have basic human needs to survive, such as food, water, and sleep. Every human needs different amounts and varieties of these things, just like different plants require different amounts of nutrients. We sometimes need more at certain times.

We know that soil can become depleted of what it needs for growth, but are you aware that depletion can also happen to your soul? If you have been living through a season that has sapped your body, mind, and soul, you must layer in self-reflection and self-care to ready yourself for growth. In your daily routine, sprinkle in questions like *How am I doing? How do I feel in my body, in my mind, and in my soul? What do I need to feel ready to grow?* Don't allow the hamster wheel of life to steal rest and recovery from your soul. You need rest *and* recovery to grow! Slow down, check in, and get more curious about how you are feeding your soul and be willing to rest and allow your soul to restore itself naturally.

#2 -*Lack of Resources* – On the farm, there is a consistent sentiment that there is simply not enough of the most important resources to make things grow: time, money, or help. Seekers pursuing growth and their Inspired Life can sometimes feel that way too. In order to prioritize yourself and your growth, think about what option suits you best. Do you want to seek the support of professionals? Do you want to take a class? Do you need help with your family responsibilities? Or would you rather step away from professional responsibilities to spend more time at home? When we are faced with so many choices and possibilities, it's easy to give into the scarcity mindset that there is never enough time, money, or help.

But the truth is that there *is* enough—most times, anyway. Just focus on that important question: *What is enough for me?* Remembering your answer to that important question will enable you to shift your perspective, realign your priorities, and encourage you to look for ways to seek support. When it comes to creating your Inspired Life, you can grow with little-to-no financial investment if you are willing to invest in yourself with time. But if you are in a financial position to invest in a business or life coach or one with the particular professional skills you need, go for it.

Even if you are planning to start classes, attend seminars, or hire a trusted coach, there's no need to wait to get started on your growth journey. All you need is this book, a pen and some paper, and a commitment to give yourself time to grow. You might even join a group of other committed Seekers to meet with regularly and inspire each other and create accountability. Get creative and set aside time to grow. Prioritize yourself—trust that you are your best resource. Learn to value and respect your time and energy, and ask for help if you need more time to spend with yourself.

#3 -*Lack of Expertise* – On any given day at the farm, my farmer-husband has to wear many hats: He has to fulfill the duties of mechanic, horticulturist, grain marketer, crop salesman, planter, fertilizer, or sower of all the seeds—it's a lot. The same will be true for you as you put on your Seeker hat and put in the work to grow. Odds are as you create your Inspired Life, you will have to try all sorts of new things. You might have to learn how to create and run a business, or find a new way to network and make connections that are vital in order to move forward, or even have to apply for a new position where you don't yet have all the required experience. Lack of expertise can feel scary and overwhelming, especially as you are trying all these new things while you are in the middle of trying to grow.

I'm here to remind you that it's okay. Don't give into the lie that you have to be the knower of all things. You can't be an expert on day one at everything you do or try. Just like all of us, you have to learn as you grow. You will learn to accept that you cannot know all things because you trust in your humble curiosity. You *will* get better at navigating and learning whatever it is you might not know because you have everyday bravery on your side. With humble curiosity, you'll learn new things yourself, outsource that learning to someone else, or partner with someone who cares about you and your growth. Simply stated, you'll trust that you aren't the only Seeker out there.

Just remember, confidence is a product of consistency and experience—disciplined consistency. Don't focus on your lack of expertise; focus on your ability and willingness to live and learn.

#4 - *Well-Worn Patterns of Behavior and Thinking* – On the farm, there's not much worse than having to drive over or out of deep ruts near the barn, in the field, or on the roads. Whether those ruts are from the constant wear and tear of heavy equipment or from natural erosion due to flowing water, when ruts run deep you can get stuck, and they are hard to get out of.

It's the same with humans. Odds are you have been doing life a certain way for a good amount of time. Since we were born, we've been learning how to live our life. We've watched our parents, we've followed societal norms, we've built our own personal and family practices—how we think and how we do what we do. That's why you might have to learn how to first recognize where you might be in one or more ruts and then how to get out of ruts that might no longer serve you. It's hard to change. I know it. But you can and will change if you keep making choice after choice to try.

Choose to see and explore with humble curiosity any well-worn ruts that you might struggle to get out of in your own life. When you find a repeated pattern of behavior or thinking that no longer serves you, it will be easy to just say, "But that's just how I've always done it." Attaining your Inspired Life requires you to abandon that reaction to get out of ruts so that you can create safer, healthier paths toward your potential. It will take time, but with everyday bravery, humble curiosity, and disciplined consistency, you'll pave new paths to your dreams.

#5 -*Competition and Comparison* – On the farm, competition includes anything that attacks the plants or crops, but it also extends to land developers or even other farmers. All those factors are competing to take up more space, more land, more resources (think water, sunshine, and livelihood) in their own attempts to survive. In those real or expected bouts of competition, it is all too easy for the farmer to choose to invest time and energy into comparing their fields to those of others. And the same goes for

Seekers. When it comes to us humans, competition and comparison can get in the way of our growth in a few ways. They include:

- Competing with ourselves and our self-imposed expectations.
- Competing with the silent or expressed expectations of others (family, friends, work, etc.).
- Competing with others directly or indirectly through comparison.

In some ways, those tendencies are natural human traits. But they're not necessarily good for us. In the end, a Seeker must believe that their Inspired Life is simply that—theirs! Theirs to dream up, theirs to create, and theirs to focus on. What others do is not relevant when you are imagining and pursuing your own dreams. When you start to feel entangled in competing with others, it's time to stop and reflect. One question you can ask yourself is: *Whose life should I be focusing on right now?* Clearly, it's YOUR life that you should be focusing on.

All too many times, competition and comparison are just another opportunity to judge yourself. *Am I the winner? Am I good enough?* Those are not the questions that true Seekers focus on. They focus on: *Am I trying? Am I dreaming? Am I living and learning? Am I experiencing joy and peace alongside challenges?* This is your life! Don't spend too much of it focused on other people who are merely participants in your lived experience. So, instead of focusing time and energy on expectations you may or may not be meeting, on what others want from you, on what others are doing with their life, shift your mindset and focus on yourself and what inspired actions you choose to take next.

See comparison as the thief of joy, and joy is essential to your growth. Parts of us are so well trained to be on alert for who is doing it bigger, better, faster, or more profitably. The invitation here is to stop making your growth about anyone else but yourself. It is 100% normal and natural to have competitive drives and spirits, but allowing the result of those competitions to take over your spirit and your worth is not the healthy way to grow.

Remember, the goal for a Seeker is to reduce the amount of energy given to focusing on others, instead focusing on your own growth. And now you have more tools to help you focus on yourself, what you want, what change you want to pursue. You've learned how to show up as a Seeker. You've crafted a Seeker Statement and dreamed up a perfect day, and now you'll be more aware when obstacles to growth start to creep into your life.

But there is one last obstacle that we must cover because it will be essential to your growth, and that obstacle is a scary one—fear.

#6 -*Fear of Change* – My husband has yet to come home and tell me how scary his work can be. I know that he's frequently loading, driving, and repairing massive pieces of heavy equipment that can crash, catch fire, or injure him in some awful way or another, so I might worry for him more than he does. But I guarantee you that fear is one of the most present obstacles in his chosen passion and profession, and that is because of this simple fact—he's human. Fear is one of the biggest obstacles for all of us, and it can literally stop us dead in our tracks, keeping us from growing. But before we go any further, let me assure you of something:

You are safe.

Take a deep breath and repeat these three simple words to yourself:

I am safe.
I am safe.
I am safe.

Nicely done. How does that feel in your body? My guess is if you actually took the breath and said those words, your heart might have slowed down and your muscles released just a bit of tension. Reminding yourself that you are safe is a powerful tool for growth and gives you the courage to show up with the everyday bravery you'll need to manage growing pains.

That's the real problem with change, right? That change is oftentimes fraught with fear, and we no longer feel safe. Fear of the unknown, fear of things not working out, or heck, even fear of things working out and changing how your life flows! But here's the thing: There's no point in fearing change because nothing in your life is permanent. *Nothing will last forever. Change is inevitable.*

Still, let's face it—change is hard.

That's why so many people don't choose to be a Seeker, because the real problem with growth is that it requires you to change. But before we go any further, let's define change.

Technically, *change is the act or instance of making someone or something different; to alter, modify, or replace something with something else, especially when that something else is newer or better.*

What's your definition of change? Change is _____. Fill in the blank with whatever word or words feel right to you.

While we innately understand what change is, it's how we

experience change that is at the heart of growth. As I've lived my own life and experienced numerous personal and professional seasons and transitions that led to things changing or becoming different, I've felt several similar sentiments. Here are a few of the ways I would have ended that sentence over the years:

Change is…

hard
risky
scary
terrifying
annoying
fear-inducing
frustrating
confusing
identity-blurring
isolating
an opportunity for failure
something to be avoided

For me, change was always something to avoid at all costs because my main goal was to stay safe and secure in who I was and what I was doing. I wanted to be on the straight, narrow, and "right" road. I had no interest in creating new paths—I was fine staying in the ruts I'd created. As the adult child of an alcoholic, I later learned that my patterns of behavior linked easily to my lived experience in a diseased home. My decisions and actions were always grounded in the goal to stay safe, not rock any boats, and choose security over risk-taking.

That was my mode until my personal and professional lives

imploded and I realized that by not changing my perspective, I had actually missed out on the chance to grow. I had chosen to sit idly by, ignoring the amazing opportunities out on the horizon in front of me, because I simply wasn't ready to embrace all that change had to offer me. Well, that is, until I chose to show up ready to try my best to grow.

When I realized that change is also an exciting experience (dare I say, exhilarating?) full of potential, the possibilities before me expanded exponentially. And even though down deep in my—and yes, your—DNA is the desire to stay in homeostasis and keep things just as they are, even if they're not all that great, the fact of life (indeed, science) is that we are constantly changing and evolving.

Fear has a real place in your life if it's protecting you from real danger or threat. But at other times, fear is nothing more than made-up, over-dramatic, anxiety-inducing stories of possible failure or demise. At those times, remember that you and your dreams are safe.

Here are a few of the possible fear-driven, imposter syndrome-ridden things that you might be telling yourself:

- You have no clue how to do whatever it is you want to do.
- You don't have the resources (money, willpower, intellect, or family support) to make it happen.
- You don't know and cannot figure out how to get from where you are to where you want to be.
- It's too hard, too complicated, too expensive, or too risky.
- You can't manage anything else new in your life; you're already juggling too much.

You think you don't know the answers (or that someone else has them), but the truth is that you know more than you think you know. That fact is a life-altering truth that can change the trajectory of your life even if you don't read one more page of this book.

Of course, I'm not saying that you know *all* there is to know. We all know that is not possible. But do I believe that you know more than you think you know? Absolutely. You have proven to yourself that you are willing to learn how to grow by buying and reading this book. You needed "something," and you went to find it.

You also know how to tap into yourself (and you'll learn even more in the next chapter about YOU-Turns) to look for guidance to move forward. Just operate from a head and heart space where you trust yourself to seek. Grow from a place of humble curiosity, everyday bravery, with a disciplined consistency. Yes, fear might pop up, but when it does, slow yourself down and trust that you are safe and you know more than you think you know.

Grace Is Required

Another truth that impacts every Seeker's experience is that *grace is required*. Grace has everything to do with growth and with understanding obstacles and managing growing pains. Giving yourself grace means limiting the amount of negative self-talk and self-criticism you pour into yourself. I'd expand the meaning of grace to include a high level of self-compassion as defined by author and professor Dr. Kristin Neff in her book *Self-Compassion: The Proven Power of Being Kind to Yourself.* She describes self-compassion as giving yourself the same kindness and care you'd give a good friend.

So, when you hit bumps in the road as you grow, remind yourself that you are a human, doing the best that you can, and you are capable of changing for the better. You are not alone in the journey toward your Inspired Life—there are others who choose to be Seekers too. Be confident that time and experience will deliver benefits to you over and over again. You will in fact live and learn. But instead of drowning in fear while you are doing it, allow yourself to swim in a pool of grace and cover yourself with self-compassion as you do all that living and learning.

Your brain believes what you tell it. So, tell yourself that you are your own best guide toward your Inspired Life and that you can manage any growing pains you experience. And if you want to make a change for the better in your life, keep telling yourself what it is you want and why.

Because in the end, here's the thing to remember—you are safe.

Take a moment now and bring your Seeker Statement back into your sights:

I want to...

because it will...

Read it one more time. Feel it. Trust it. Begin to believe it. I can hardly emphasize enough how important it will be to frequently repeat to yourself the "what and why" of your journey. We know that change is scary, that risk-taking is dicey. Growing from one way of doing, being, and thinking to another is hard. Yet, growth trumps fear. You deserve to live a life focused on possibility and inspired action—not one where you settle and allow fear to hold you back. So, you have to keep your vision in the front of your mind to help you keep your commitment to growth.

How You Spot a Growing Pain

The best way to spot an incoming obstacle or a growing pain is to keep checking in with yourself. If you start to feel afraid or uneasy, simply stay alert to how you are feeling and how you are responding to change—in your mind, in your body, and in your soul. Raising your awareness is key for any Seeker. Once you've become more aware of your lived experience through change, you'll have choices about what to do with that information. Invest in yourself and your growth with a few stolen minutes of self-reflection throughout your day.

Ask yourself questions like:

- *How am I feeling mentally, emotionally, or physically as I show up as a Seeker?*
- *Does anything I'm growing through feel really hard? If so, why do I think it's challenging me? Are there any new things I could try to see if it works better for me?*
- *Is there anything clearly getting in the way of progress toward my Inspired Life? If so, what are some ways I might*

remove that obstacle and/or change my pattern of thinking or behaving?

- *Are there people or places that do not support my growth? If so, can I have candid conversations to ask for support, or do I need to create and express clear boundaries (i.e., what is okay, what is not okay, and what will happen if they can't honor my requests)?*

By giving yourself time to reflect you are going to learn so much about yourself from yourself. As a Seeker, you'll build a practice of turning inward to help you find your next steps forward. And with the YOU-Turns right around the corner, you will soon be well versed and equipped with how to trust that you are in fact your own best guide through growth. But first, let's add in another Tool for Practice, to help you have a little fun managing growing pains with powerful messages filled with and fueled by hope.

In this Tool for Practice, write clear messages to yourself. Words matter, just like you matter. And now that you've started expressing yourself honestly and with more intention, it never hurts to have actual words that matter in your line of sight as you go about your day-to-day life. You are undertaking a change for the better, a change that is going to require you to venture outside your comfort zone. You are going to face obstacles along the way. But you want to keep growing. So, as you do that, one of the best people to give you a power-it-up kind of pep talk, an 'atta-girl, or a swift kick in the pants is actually YOU.

For this invitation, you simply stop and reflect on what you need to see, hear, and think in order to stay focused on your growth journey. Maybe you just want to memorize your Seeker Statement so that you remember what you want and why it matters. It's a beautiful thing to be reminded of! Or maybe there is some other mantra or phrase that is repeating itself in your mind from your Dream Day Exercise or other ideas around your Inspired Life. Whatever speaks to you, simply grab a sticky note and write it down.

Then take that power message and stick it wherever you know you'll catch a glimpse of it frequently. Over the years, I've put such notes up on my bathroom mirror, on the dash of the car, inside the kitchen cabinets, the laptop, computer monitor, or back of my office doors. No matter where you post it, the purpose is to keep meaningful words in your actual and mind's eye as you keep growing. Those messages have said all sorts of things but have served one purpose—to express myself honestly, to trust what I need to hear, and to keep those words that matter in my mind.

And to get you thinking about what you might write down, here's a sampling of my power messages:

Yes, sometimes there is a little yelling in my use of all caps, but each note includes words that I need to see, hear, and say as I venture through whatever I'm experiencing at that time.

If you have a hard time thinking of what to jot down, try this—take a few deep breaths, close your eyes, and ask yourself this question: *What do I need to hear most?*

Give yourself time to see what you hear. Don't judge whatever it might be. Just simply notice it, and if it feels right, write it out and post that power message in a place you know you'll see it with hopeful anticipation of what is to come. Remember: Your brain believes what you tell it. Tell it what it needs to hear and continue to build your Seeker-self up as you manage the growing pains you will face.

Now that you have a tool to practice building yourself up as you manage growing pains, let's remind ourselves of the facts. The choice to be a Seeker is always yours to make. Creating your Inspired Life is the single most exciting opportunity of your lifetime. Growing toward your Inspired Life won't be easy. You will face obstacles. But you know that you have choices to help you manage any growing pains that life throws your way.

So far in this section, we've spent our time and energy on planting seeds of truth and knowledge about what is possible for you and your life, so before we move on and learn how to grow in the next section, we have one final, yet vital thing to focus on—YOU! It's time to learn how to create a practice of turning back toward yourself time and time again through five distinct and powerful **YOU-Turns.**

I hope you are ready, because it's time to focus on Y-O-U!

Chapter 4

PRIORITIZE YOUR GROWTH
WITH YOU–TURNS

O nce a seed has been planted, there is so much left unseen. And in my opinion, so much underappreciated effort for the daunting work that each and every seed faces. I imagine those little seeds thinking to themselves, *What the heck do I do now? Which way do I grow?*

Here's the thing: I believe that uncertainty is the same for us humans. Something in us knows it wants to grow, but no one tells us how to create an active, loving relationship with our soul. And we need to create a loving and trusting connection so that we can help usher it through all the growth that it longs to have, all the impact it wants to make, and all the life it wants to experience!

The problem is actually two-fold. First, we aren't taught to tend to our soul. Second, we mistakenly prioritize the wrong things and lose track of ourselves. We need all the tools in our growth toolkit to help us understand how we can best grow. If we don't have them, we spin our wheels trying but not truly moving forward. We end up feeling stuck, lost, alone, or hopeless. Why?

Because we've lost track of the most important thing—ourselves.

Tending to our own needs by prioritizing ourselves is fundamental to growth. Nevertheless, I know from the women who tell me they listen to my podcast, attend my events, or work with me as a life coach that the prioritizing aspect is where many women start to feel uncomfortable. The idea of prioritizing themselves and their personal growth and development feels foreign, or even worse, unacceptable. But remember: To grow is to live. We all have to grow. And we can't grow without prioritizing ourselves. The concept can seem scary sometimes, but that is only because we have so often been trained to seek and serve others first. We pride ourselves on being selfless caregivers for others. It's okay that we all long to be good wives, mothers, business owners, and community members, but while doing all of those things for all of the people, we have to remember ourselves.

Prioritizing yourself is not only necessary, it's the only way to build a solid and healthy foundation for life-giving growth. The Seeker way of living and being—the way of *choosing to try and seek change for the better*—is the ultimate act of self-devotion. Choosing this brave way of growing is not selfish. It is never to the neglect of others. It is the most beautiful choice you can make for yourself and anyone else you "do" life with.

Choosing to accept the invitation to befriend change and evolve day in and day out affords you the opportunity to joyously create the Inspired Life of your dreams, lovingly embrace the seasons of your life, and grow as you go!

But first, let me remind you of another important fact.

You are a leader.

I need you to hear me. Read these next words slowly and take them to heart.

YOU ARE A LEADER. (Sorry to yell, but it's so important.)

In her book *Dare to Lead*, Brené Brown defines a leader as anyone who holds themselves accountable for finding potential in people and processes, and who has the courage to develop that potential. That is who you are... the *freaking leader of your own freaking life*. And more than that, you've chosen to be a Seeker—a *leader* who shows up day in and day out choosing to seek change for the better, ready to pursue *your* potential armed with humble curiosity, everyday bravery, and disciplined consistency.

Being a leader truly takes commitment, but all of us are human, and we all have very normal and natural tendencies to *not* prioritize ourselves. That's why it's time that we focus on the **+** part of the powerful, life-changing equation:

The Growth Cycle **+ YOU-Turns** = *An Inspired Life*

Remember that the goal of this book is for you to learn how to create YOUR Inspired Life. We've spent time planting new powerful seeds of knowledge about what it means to be a Seeker and how important it is to choose the Seeker lifestyle. We've also focused time and energy learning how to dream up your Inspired Life. And since we know that this is not easy work, we planted other seeds of awareness when it comes to obstacles and how to manage growing pains that might spring up along the way.

But now it's time to look at what is needed to nurture your soul throughout the cycles of growth that make up your life. Nurturing your own soul as you move along your own path of growth requires *you* learning how to prioritize *yourself*. It does not mean putting yourself ahead of *everything else*; it means becoming accustomed to turning in and back toward yourself time and time again as needed, remembering your goal of creating and living an Inspired Life—one that you are excited about, eager to wake up for, and committed to pursuing even in the face of struggle. Prioritizing yourself takes constant and consistent YOU-Turns.

What Is a YOU-Turn

YOU-Turns are the totally essential, yet completely untaught, tools of self-reflection that allow us to grow. YOU-Turns are where we learn to shift our focus back in and toward ourselves when we find ourselves lost or stuck in what others think, what others are doing, or what others are telling us (explicitly or not) to do. YOU-Turns are the shifts in perspective that help us create a lasting, loving relationship with our soul built on time, trial and error, and trust.

YOU-Turns are all about *you* and how you ask *yourself* what *you* need. YOU-Turns are how you learn to honor those needs. They are also options for action to meet those needs as best you can with the information, wisdom, and discernment you have available to you.

YOU-Turns don't ignore others—they simply allow you to connect with yourself FIRST before bringing in others, learning to trust that you can in fact lead yourself (because remember you know more than you think you know). Sometimes, the YOU-turn will prompt you to seek help, guidance, and support from others. Each YOU-Turn you experience can look different depending on the circumstances. But no matter when you use them, YOU-Turns are essential tools to have in your toolkit before diving into understanding and navigating the Growth Cycle.

YOU-Turns are moments where you stop and check in with

yourself to see how you're feeling, ask what you might need, and give yourself the attention you deserve. YOU-Turns work to free us when we are trapped in our own unhealthy, nonproductive patterns of thinking, doing, or being.

YOU-Turns keep you on track when you are faced with the challenges that will inevitably arise. That's why you use the YOU-Turns to reconnect with the leader of your Inspired Life (ahem, that's YOU!) and give yourself time and space to identify your next inspired steps forward. You want to feel in your bones that your next steps are the right next steps for you. And you want to know that you have given yourself time in self-reflection to have peace in your decisions for action. That's exactly what the YOU-Turns allow you to do.

When growing gets challenging—as it inevitably will at times—you can use these five YOU-Turns repeatedly to help reconnect to yourself and find your next inspired steps forward. Each YOU-Turn serves as a possible course correction when you feel like you've lost your way or don't even know where to begin. Remember, by turning inward with a YOU-Turn, you give yourself time to reorient your thinking and find the free-to-grow feeling you long for as you navigate the phases of the Growth Cycle that we'll cover in the next section of this book.

Let's dig in and discuss each YOU-Turn available to you when you feel disconnected from your soul as it tries to grow:

YOU-Turn 1: Trust that you matter. We all have undeniable needs for love, connection, and significance. We want our lives to matter. But all too many times we look externally for proof that we matter rather than genuinely trusting that it is a fact—you matter. Even without titles and material possessions, awards and praise, you matter!

I know how wonderful it feels to have someone praise you for work you've done. But I challenge you to see how it feels when you are truly proud of yourself, without relying on praise from others on the outside. You should be proud of yourself not for what you can produce or accomplish or for the title next to your name, but simply because you are a living, breathing person with a soul that longs to find meaning and purpose while you're still here. That alone is reason to celebrate!

Simply say these words out loud: *I trust that I matter.* Or if you're worn out, narrow it down to two words for one killer fact: *I matter.* Stop trying to prove your worth or finding validation in titles and labels and instead choose to celebrate your existence, appreciating and accepting the unique essence you bring to the world.

Trust that you matter. Stop trying to earn the right to be you. Stop trying to prove your worth. Choose to show up with the humble curiosity, everyday bravery, and disciplined consistency that is calling your name, whispering... ready or not... it's time to try, and it's time to grow.

YOU-Turn 2: Listen to your voice. You are an endless well of knowledge, and over time you will build a stronger sense of trust in your gut and intuition by asking yourself questions and patiently waiting for responses. You will trust your body and mind to guide yourself as no one else can.

The truth is that you know more than you think you know, so trust yourself. You have to hold confidence that your ideas, thoughts, opinions, and instincts matter! Stop listening to "they" or "them" and the unconscious callings of societal norms. Instead, listen to your gut, trust your intuition, and share your voice from your perspective.

It's normal to battle expectations that are imposed upon you or created in your own mind (remember all those stories you tell yourself?). We all do this at times, but it is not helpful. This YOU-Turn is an option to slow down and give yourself time, especially in moments of decision, to ask yourself: *Is this really what I want? Is it right for me? Do I want to grow this way?* Then trust the steady, calm voice that answers you. And if it's garbled or full of lots of words—you might not be ready to make a decision. And that's okay. Let time take time before rushing forward.

If tuning into your voice does not come naturally to you, the only way to get better is to do it more. Listening to your voice is a YOU-Turn you can tap into over and over again. When you're first starting to use it, make the practice as simple as taking a deep breath, closing your eyes, and saying to yourself or out loud, "I'm here, and I'm listening." Show up with everyday bravery and start the conversation with yourself and your gut. Let it know you are there and see how over time you can hear more and more of what your soul is longing to tell you.

YOU-Turn 3: Share your sh!t (or stuff if you need the PG version). This YOU-Turn is a healthy means of processing your growth and the challenges you will inevitably face. Way too many times we adopt the "fake it until you make it" mentality, even while we might really be struggling. We bottle up our thoughts, feelings, and fears, and put on a smile to pretend that it's fine, you're fine, everything is fine. The truth is that everything will not always be fine, and we need to let our soul vent.

I am a woman of many, many words, so it's not surprising that

I like to share them with others, especially when I've hit a rough patch. But even my husband of far, far fewer words needs to process his world and connect with others who might be able to support him—everyone does! That's why it's important to stop pretending that everything is "fine" and choose to be kind, open, and real with yourself and others. Process and share your authentic life experience with trusted confidantes. Note I didn't say to share your business with anyone who will listen—that's not safe or healthy. Look around you for other Seekers or people in your trusted community and see who might be able to lend a listening ear.

If you're struggling, share it. If you're killing it and torn on what to tackle next, share it. If you are growing but it's impacting important relationships and not for the better, share that sh!t. This YOU-Turn carries a risk of letting others know you don't have it all together all of the time. But remember: Nobody does! Sharing is the best option to connect with someone else and remind yourself that you are not alone, that you can listen to your voice and your soul's need to process its reality, and share your kind, open, and real-life truth with others who have earned the right to hear it.

YOU-Turn 4: Ask for help. You are not meant to grow alone. Seekers do not hold too tightly to the "I got this!" mentality, because they know at times that they will not be able to do it all, be it all, or accomplish it all. Seekers use this YOU-Turn to remind themselves that other people love them and might be able to help and support them. See the honor in asking for help, knowing that someday you might be the one to help others as they grow.

Not asking for help simply hustles our way into martyrdom. Women are more prone to this mindset than are men, but dudes can also hold tight to the need to prove that they are capable, grown men who can perform and provide, all on their own. That's why this YOU-turn implores that you stop trying to prove your worth by doing it alone. Instead, it encourages you to ask for help when you are struggling to get little things done OR big things that are weighing you down.

You might seek counsel from family, friends, or heck, even from strangers (but not just any stranger). As a firm believer in the power of professional support, I have sought out a number of counselors and therapists in my lifetime, and each has served me in times when I knew I needed that support. Depending on your lived experience, you might have more or less emotional weight to wade through and process. Whether for general growth purposes or for emotional cases, don't reject the assistance of someone who is trained in those areas as needed.

Another challenge that can arise is that many of your tightly held beliefs about your worth might be called into question. Many learned behavior patterns might not feel safe or productive anymore. You might notice that relationships start to experience distress or suffer as you grow, leaving others unsteady, unappreciative, or simply scared about the "new you."

All those changes are normal. If you feel you are struggling and not wanting to ask for help, please think back to all the other YOU-Turns and listen to and trust that voice within, which might be asking for help. Keep in mind that the best place to share your stuff might be with a professional.

YOU-Turn 5: Explore your options. By exploring more, you will find what works for you, what doesn't, and what you might try next. Trust that the unknown before you will ultimately serve you for the good of your growth. This YOU-Turn helps to reorient your thinking from believing that there is only one way to grow or that someone else's way must be the right way. Let your outlook turn to the truth that the only way for you to know is to try. And try lots of things because there are in fact tons of options available to you.

This YOU-Turn is all about getting better at believing that *you can't know unless you try.*

Exploring your options might be particularly useful if or when you find yourself frustrated or maybe even bored as you choose to keep seeking growth. Avoid living vicariously through others' social media or holding yourself back from new learnings that interest you because they don't seem to be popular subjects. Instead of living in a constant state of FOMO (that darn fear of missing out), choose to try something new for yourself, to push slightly outside the limits of your comfort zone. As we work through the phases of the Growth Cycle and in your growth, exploring many options will serve you well in all aspects of your life—spiritual, emotional, physical, and intellectual.

Remember that the most important way to stay unstuck is to try new things as a curious explorer of your own life. *You can't know unless you try.* Surprise yourself with what you can live and learn. Play with your options and find what excites you and brings you some well-deserved joy! And if something doesn't feel good or is a definite "No, thank you, never again," then celebrate that you learned something new about your soul and move on. To put it simply, listen to and trust your gut to be your growth guide.

For me, I always said I wanted to have a podcast, but I couldn't have known if I'd really like it, not to mention whether I'd enjoy the process in order to devote time and energy to it, unless I tried it myself. So, I did. You can find my podcast *You Just Don't Know*

It Yet, which I co-host with my dear friend Wendy, on Spotify and iTunes. We talk about motherhood, friendship, and all real-life related topics. I was so nervous to try podcasting, but lo and behold, it turns out to be something that gives me a creative outlet and one that means more to me than how many downloads it gets. And I wouldn't have even known that unless I tried, put it out in the world, and learned how I felt about it all.

On the other hand, I recently agreed to compete in a women's-only mud obstacle course race. Yeah, a race that is called MUDGIRL where we'd literally be covered in mud. I already knew I enjoyed obstacle course races, but I had no way of knowing that I really, really didn't like getting dirty until I showed up, slogged my way through, and had to hose off in the Texas sun. There was no way I could know that unless I tried. But now I know. No more mud races for me!

So, use this YOU-Turn as a way to test out the limits of your comfort zone. It doesn't matter how other people feel about things and what they recommend as the next right move for you. You have to explore and experience them for yourself to help find your next steps forward.

As you have read, all five YOU-Turns are designed to get *you* where *you* want to go. Self-directed growth will require a whole new level of self-validation that many of us have not tapped into because we were never taught. It's not easy work. Most if not all of us were taught to seek approval from others, to earn our way forward, to prove that we are worthy because someone else gives us a green light. But there is a better way! Self-validation is not only a powerful tool in growth but also a confidence-building gift of growth. Don't ever underestimate the power of seeing, believing, and affirming yourself!

As you keep practicing, you'll get more and more comfortable trusting yourself through the growth process. It takes time, lived experience, and a steady stream of reminders that you are in fact the best, most qualified leader of your own life. And my hopeful wish is that you will pull out, like the pesky weeds they are, some of the patterns of people-pleasing, self-doubting, and fear-limiting behaviors that might stand in the way of your growth. Remember, *you* are in fact in control of your life—you alone, regardless of your salary or title, regardless of your role as mom/dad/spouse/life partner, business owner, community leader, etc. *You* will come to a point where your identity is no longer linked to what you do, but rather about how you consistently show up ready to grow.

You Are Your Best Guide to Growth

Let me admit something to you: My husband is an amazing man and an excellent farmer. His knowledge about seed germination is extraordinary. But, in my opinion, like I shared earlier his comment that the seed's work is easier than the farmer's is simply not true.

When it comes to humans—you and me—we have a seed that was planted in us. And that seed is our soul. It longs to grow. It longs to have meaning and purpose. And while the seed and plant will never be able to tell my farmer-hubby what it needs, as humans, we have a wildly active soul that is trying to talk to us.

Sarah Blondin, mother, artist, writer, and podcast host, penned a beautiful meditation called *Things I Wish Someone Had Told Me* that perfectly summarizes what I too wish someone had told me when I started my growth journey. I highly encourage you to find it on your own device and give yourself the time to listen to her wisdom in its entirety. But a few lines rang so deep and true and highlight why YOU-Turns are essential. I want to share them with you here:

> *I wish someone had told me when I first began my journey into a life of my own that where I needed to begin was sitting on the floor, with my eyes closed. I wish someone had told me that my first step, the first step anyone must take is inward.*

I could have definitely used her words before my life imploded years back. But the truth is without my own life crisis I would never have had the chance to choose me. I chose to turn in toward myself over and over again. And in doing so I fell in love with myself for the first time—simply because I chose to prioritize myself. I chose to give myself time.

Here is another Tool for Practice to give you an opportunity to turn toward yourself and develop a deeper understanding of who you are and how you want to show up for your Inspired Life.

YOUR PERSONAL MANIFESTO

A Personal Manifesto is a written declaration of your core values and beliefs as well as a place to outline how you intend to live your life. It is a deeply personal and unique opportunity to clarify for yourself who you are, what you believe, what you value and why, and how you want to bring all of your values to life through your actions. This tool provides your first opportunity to think deeper and go further than a Seeker Statement and can serve you as a daily mantra, touchpoint, or grounding phrase. Both your Seeker Statement and whatever magic came from your Dream Day Exercise can serve as the initial basis of your Personal Manifesto. If you say in your Seeker Statement that you want what you want, what you write in your Personal Manifesto should be in alignment with that. If you have a Dream Day in mind, your Personal Manifesto should build out the ways of thinking, doing, and being that will support you on your way to making that dream your reality.

Where the Seeker Statement and Dream Day Exercise help you home in what you want (a mission statement, if you will) and help you have a solid vision in your mind's eye (a true-life vision statement), the Personal Manifesto serves as a place for you to expound on what it will take for you to get there. Think of it as more of an operating manual. The accountant in me, for example, couldn't grow without a few policies and procedures documented for me to live by. Likewise, a Personal Manifesto contains your "operating manual" to live by.

This Tool for Practice might take you five minutes, five hours, or five days as you read the following questions then weed through your beliefs and get them out of your head and onto paper or in an online document. And if you've never attempted to document these things for yourself, don't fret. Remember there are no right or wrong answers. You never have to share it with anyone unless you choose to. Don't worry about getting it exactly right, because it can and most likely will change some over time as you gain new insight and wisdom.

What this manifesto will offer you, though, is a place to come back to when you face the challenges of change. It will remind you of who you are and what you are about. It will remind you that even if you don't have all the answers, you do know certain things about who you are and how you want to live your life. These pronouncements work best too if you write in the present tense (e.g., I explore my options with curiosity), stay positive (because all of these things are for the good!), use strong language (write it like you really, really mean it), and try to keep it short, sweet, and simple. It should be a declaration that you are likely to check and recheck, so it's very helpful to read it often.

Here is a list of questions to prompt your musings:

* Who am I?

* What do I believe?

* What core values guide my behaviors?

* What inspires me or brings me joy?

* What things do I limit or avoid because they do not serve me well (mentally, spiritually, emotionally, physically)?

* How will I take care of myself (mind, body, and soul)?

* How will I treat others?

* How will I expect others to treat me?

* What will I do with my time and energy?

* How will living by this manifesto impact me and others?

* What legacy do I long to leave?

Your Personal Manifesto matters, just like you matter. I remember typing my own manifesto years ago and safely saving it on my computer. I try to go back to it annually and see how things might need to change, what still feels spot on, and to remind myself of what I should give my time, energy, and effort to. I suggest you do the same, although probably more frequently as you start growing.

Save your manifesto in a place you won't forget and set reminders in your calendar to go back to it. Allow it to be another tool to support your efforts to create your Inspired Life. All the answers you need to grow toward your Inspired Life and to live that life in alignment with your Personal Manifesto are inside you. If something you have said you want doesn't align with your manifesto, stop and think about whether a change needs to be made. Use your manifesto to check in as you make YOU-Turns.

At this point, I hope that your chest is puffing out just a bit with pride for all you've learned so far, all you've decided to believe you are capable of creating. You know that growth is a long-haul game and that you'll have to manage growing pains. But now that you are armed with five fundamental YOU-Turns, you will turn in and toward yourself as you navigate the growth toward your Inspired Life as well as be better prepared for challenges that always tend to sneak up on you (thanks, life).

But now that we've planted those new seeds in your heart, soul, and mind, it's time to *grow*!

Grow

SHIFTING SOIL

ROOTING TRUST

THE *Growth* CYCLE

BREAKING THROUGH

PACING PURSUIT

Chapter 5

GROWTH CYCLE PHASE 1

SHIFTING SOIL

Why are you here?

Tell me—and remind yourself quickly—why did you pick up this book? My guess is that you had a longing in your heart for change. But now that we've spent time looking into what that means, let me ask you this: *What does your Inspired Life look like? What do you want to keep growing toward? How did you incorporate these longings in your Seeker Statement?* Remind yourself of them now:

I want to...

because it will...

In the first section of the book—*Plant*—you read each page and planted new seeds of what is possible for you and your life. The seeds contained hope and awareness, prompting you to focus on the far side of the equation I've shared—an Inspired Life. You also learned why it is so important that you choose to be a Seeker. Armed with a Seeker's mindset, you practiced dreaming up your one-of-a-kind Inspired Life. Then together we focused on what can and will try to get in the way of your growth. You learned how to identify and manage those growing pains you might (okay, will) experience.

Then in Chapter 4, we focused on how you can better connect with yourself, reorient your thinking, and prioritize yourself as you make changes for the better. We learned that this process will require you to turn back toward yourself time and time again with one or all of the YOU-Turns available to you. At each YOU-Turn, you used your Seeker's humble curiosity, everyday bravery, and disciplined consistency to help you trust yourself and grow more confident in your own ability to be your very own best guide.

Now, in this second section of the book—*Grow*—we will focus on how we cycle through change time and again toward the growth we long for. For the next several chapters, it's time that we focus on how our hearts, souls, and very busy minds navigate the four phases of a very consistent and reliable Growth Cycle. While keeping your vision of your Inspired Life in mind, you'll use the YOU-Turns as a bedrock for connecting to yourself as well to weather each challenging Growth Cycle you venture through.

The math remains simple, and it's time we focus on the final component of the equation:

The Growth Cycle + *YOU-Turns* = *An Inspired Life*

When you understand the phases of the Growth Cycle, you will become more in tune with yourself and the opportunities to live, learn, and most importantly, keep growing. The Growth Cycle is an ever-repeating process that will look different at each interval in terms of the specific change, transition, or challenge you face. But regardless of what you're dealing with in your life, you'll pass through four different phases: Shifting Soil, Breaking Through, Pacing Pursuit, and Rooting Trust.

Each phase has its own unique challenges and opportunities. By understanding each phase, you will better be able to identify how to best navigate your own path toward a more evolved version of you. All growth experiences are different, but as you will see, no matter who we are or what we are dealing with, there is a common cycle of growth. By knowing where you might be in the Growth Cycle or what phase might be on the horizon, you can keep growing with more calm, confidence, and grace.

So, let's dig in to the first phase of the Growth Cycle—Shifting Soil.

What Is Shifting Soil

Imagine a plant that has sprouted out of the earth. Maybe it's a sunflower, or a bean stalk if vegetables are more your thing. It might be just one tiny stalk, or it could be a plant that's had time to grow decent roots and has leaves that blow in the wind. Now think back to science class in elementary school. As I'm sure you've learned, the plant consists of much more than just what you can see above the ground. We all know there is a system below the dirt that grows toward gravity and holds the plant firmly in place—the roots.

But what we don't think about much is how the roots grow in soil that moves—hence the term "Shifting Soil." The soil all around the roots is constantly (though imperceptibly) moving. Therefore, the ground in which the plant is growing, the same ground where it holds itself safe and sound in its little piece on this planet, is always changing—just like the plant itself. And the plant has to respond to the changing conditions around it, meaning it has to feel the rub and respond to that disturbance of its rooted peace.

The concept of Shifting Soil is no different for us humans. Just like the soil shifts underground, invisibly to us, you too will have to deal with how to respond to any unrest you might feel as your soul is trying to grow. Many of us choose to ignore those shifts. But since you are a Seeker at heart, I trust that you will keep reading to learn more about how the shifting soil is nothing but an indication that you are on the right path. Growth is coming!

Shifting Soil is the first phase of the Growth Cycle—a discomfort, frustration, rub—in your soul. If you fail to give it attention, you might end up with big cracks in the foundation of your life. The Shifting Soil phase of the Growth Cycle is when you finally hear the whispers inside your mind that call for change in your life.

I'm here to remind you that if we listen closely enough, each of us has the guidance within us that will help us persevere in our growth despite the ground shifting beneath us. Just pay attention! Whatever you want to call it—your gut, your intuition, your internal knowing—wants your attention as you grow. Are you ready to listen?

How to Know You've Entered the Shifting Soil Phase

Shifting Soil begins when you start to realize that you long for and need change in your life. It's the beginning of real change, but remember that in this early stage, you might not yet have all the answers you need. You simply have something within you saying you want or need something new in your life.

Let me be real with you: This first phase of the Growth Cycle can be frustrating because we know something doesn't feel right, but we don't exactly know what to do about it. That lack of clarity causes many of us to delay taking action. Maybe this sounds a little familiar to you? We can be paralyzed by fear of the unknown. That makes sense; it is natural for humans to want answers before acting. It's not comfortable sitting in uncertainty. We want a plan, and preferably a simple, pain-free, quick, and easy way to get from Point A to Point B. Society has trained us to look for the easy way out of pain or undesired circumstances and offers us every chance to buy our way to happiness with quick fixes. But the changes we're looking to make here won't necessarily come easily. That's why they can be a bit scary!

Our natural fear of change is what leads us to, in so many cases, not take the action we need and instead become paralyzed in doubt. While it is a natural and normal response to change and the uncertainty it brings, that mindset keeps us from achieving the growth we need.

I'm here to tell you this: Just like the shifting soil under the little bean plant, you and your dreams are safe. Change doesn't destroy them. In fact, it's part of the necessary process of making them come true! If you can hold that concept close to your heart, then you'll start to recognize that you're in the phase of Shifting

Soil. It can be exciting! It is full of little hints from your subconscious, showing you that there is a better path forward, one that's more authentically you. The only way to grow through this first phase, feel the ground shift beneath you, is to also hold to this truth: You have *options*.

There is not only one way to grow. If you could see beneath the soil, not one set of roots looks the same or grows the same. Just like for plants and trees, each of us grows our own way, not to mention multiple ways to grow at any given time. So, when you enter into a phase of Shifting Soil, it's time to trust that you have options to explore with humble curiosity. Let's continue to bring this concept to life.

What Shifting Soil Looks and Feels Like

In choosing to grow as a Seeker, you'll gradually release your grip on certainty and security and instead choose to focus on curiosity. You'll learn to trust in the ever-repeating Growth Cycle, which will give you a sense of peace in the process of changing.

Learning to trust your voice and recognize that the time has come for change is a personal endeavor. As you undertake that endeavor, remember you are equipped with free will to make choices for yourself that honor the messages you are hearing about your life, the little whispers or the loud shouts that are telling you now is the time to make a change. And by believing there are many ways to live your life and by approaching what you want and know (or don't yet know) with curiosity, you shift your mindset to one not focused on any "right way" to do things, but rather *your* way of doing them.

It can and will take time to process any shifts in your life. It's not easy or quick. Here's what happened to me: In the second year of my 15-year career in public accounting, I was sitting at my desk, my mind buried in a spreadsheet when something inside me whispered—*this is not going to be the profession for you.* That was it, just a quick thought that dashed through my mind and started a rub in my heart. It felt right and true but also seemed absurd to go and leave to do anything else. I simply had no bandwidth or belief that I had other options. But I couldn't completely silence that little voice. A few months later, I shared what I'd been thinking with one of my team members as we were holed up in a dimly lit office commiserating over our less than fulfilling professional endeavors.

"I don't think I can do this forever," I blurted. "What are you going to do?" I asked him.

"I don't know, maybe start a restaurant focused on grilled cheese," he responded, staring at the wall in front of him, trying to make his hazy future a bit clearer. "What about you?" he shot back.

"I don't know either. But whatever it is, I want to talk to people."

Our dreams were clear as mud, weren't they? Now, in hindsight I can see that this uncertainty was totally normal. We were in the Shifting Soil phase, when a little voice inside us was alerting us that we needed change and needed to be willing to put up with some level of discomfort to get our growth started. We also found from that conversation that we were willing to share our sh!t and talk things out as we tried to process what we really wanted for ourselves. Amazing! I didn't even know that I was using that important YOU-Turn back then.

And sure enough, 13 years later, I finally made my shift into podcasting, producing women's events, life coaching, speaking, and writing books. My team member (whom I consider a friend)... well, he didn't stay in the Shifting Soil nearly as long. A few months later when he had returned from his honeymoon, he quit his accounting job and opened a successful cheese shop with his wife—Antonelli's Cheese Shop. Their business mission is "Do Good. Eat Good." They are living, breathing proof to me that to truly build the Inspired Life you long for, you have to first honor the Shifting Soil.

I'm telling you this story so you can see that just like myself and my former coworker, you will not have all the answers when you go through this first phase of the Growth Cycle. But you will have an inkling that it's time to grow—and you should listen to it. Don't wait for guarantees of success as you make changes for the better, but choose to believe down to your core that you know more than you think you know. Both will guarantee that you will grow in the process.

Remember that you are your own best guide, even though it can already be frightening to know in your own heart that you are longing for a change. I know that charging into that change alone can be downright daunting, regardless of how many months or years it takes to begin. I remember one time I felt just like that.

One evening years back, my husband and I sat side by side at the kitchen table. We were discussing my next steps as I prepared for my professional transition out of accounting and into entrepreneurship. I was still wading through the Shifting Soil phase for sure, and I remember yelling, either in my mind or maybe even out loud to him, "Just tell me what to do!"

Wait, what? I wanted someone to tell me what to do? To make the decisions for me? That demand was very out of character. I was a partner in an amazing accounting firm. I was highly regarded by my team and peers. I had a history of success, a couple of college degrees, and a solid career to prove I was a smart, capable woman. So, why did I feel like I needed someone else to guide me forward?

The truth is, I was asking for direction from someone else because I was freaking out. I had known since year two of my 15-year career that I wanted a change—but I had held those whispers at bay. Finally, they turned to shouts, and I knew I had to leave accounting. I knew there was something better, bigger, and more meaningful out there with my name on it. But at that moment, with the soil shifting beneath me, fear had gnawed a hole in my heart and I simply couldn't handle not knowing what to do, how to do it, or how to maneuver this big decision. I wanted someone to tell me what to do, and at that moment, that someone was my husband. I figured he could make the choice for me, and I could follow instructions. I could avoid my fear by simply allow-ing someone else to guide the way, making the choices for me. His direction would make everything easier and more straightforward. I eagerly waited for him to tell me what he thought my next steps should be.

Except the response I got back from my husband was…

"Only *you* can do this, Dena."

I sat quietly absorbing his response, frustrated, yet knowing he was right. Instead of giving the clarity and certainty I longed for, he put the onus squarely back on me. He reminded me that I had a choice to make—would I keep looking outside of myself or choose to make a YOU-Turn and focus on my own intuition as my guide? It was a reminder that I am in fact in charge of my own choices in life. So dang it, if I say I want something, if I feel it in my heart and soul, then I will eventually have to trust that the longings of my heart matter, believe that I matter, and that I can't know unless I try. And the same goes for you—Shifting Soil is all about turning inward and listening to the voice, your voice that is longing to tell you something really important. So, listen up.

Finally, let me share one more story to remind you of something else that is essential to this phase of the Growth Cycle. As you work through your Shifting Soil, you'll have to trust in the fact that you have options. I once sat with one of my coaching clients, Marla, as we considered her next steps forward toward her personal and professional goal of finding more peace and balance. She had owned and operated her own business successfully for decades but was longing to make changes for the better that she simply hadn't been able to do on her own.

She came to me and explained as best she could how she was feeling and why she'd reached out to me. She'd been feeling frustrated, near hopeless, persistently pessimistic, and only sure of one thing—that she doubted her ability to change.

I rattled off several options she had when it came to making change. These included seemingly small things like rethinking her calendar, where she directed her energy, what she devoted time to, or blocking off times where she would not respond to client emails. Then I mentioned some larger things like creating a three-month action plan, hiring additional staff or consultants to offload tasks, or investing in a kickass she-shed to move her work outside her home. She sat for a second, seemingly perplexed, then she asked:

"I can do that?"

"Umm, yeah, you can do that. Or you can read another book about business restructuring, or meet with another practitioner to talk about how they plan for retirement, or go to a networking event, or fire some of the clients that don't bring you joy. There are lots of ways to do what you want to do, to honor what your gut is telling you, which is that it's time to make a change for the better."

As she grew through this phase of the Growth Cycle, it wasn't about making the changes she wanted instantly. It was about acknowledging that she wanted something better for herself. It was about giving her feelings of frustration a voice and sharing her reality and dreams for change with me. Ultimately, through time in our coaching sessions, she was able to shift her thinking and believe that she *did have options* and *she could figure things out if she'd be willing to try.* She has changed her whole lens on life from one that was full of despair that things could never change to one full of possibility.

Nearly a year after we started working together, we met for coffee one morning, and I'll never forget her saying to me: "The entire way driving over here, all I saw were options."

Her personal transformation was powerful to watch, but how can *you* work through any internal whispers you are hearing, alerting you to shifting soil in your life? How can *you* open your eyes to the endless options available to you? I'll tell you how: You choose to stay curious.

Stay Curious

You are reading this book because you want to make a change for the better in your life. You may or may not have a plan yet because you might just be giving time and energy to the shifts in your soul. This period might feel unnerving. Deep down, you want to pursue a different way of living, being, or doing. But you don't know the exact path to get there.

You have a flutter in your stomach, a whisper in your mind, a repeating daydream, or a clanging cymbal alerting you to something you want or don't want in your life. Can you stay curious and remain in that shifting soil? Or will you get lost in the trap of clinging to safety or certainty, ultimately impeding your own roots from spreading and your leaves from seeking the sunlight they need? That's the choice and—spoiler alert—*choosing curiosity is the key.*

Curiosity will be the key for you to imagine various ways to make your desires become your reality. Curiosity is the secret sauce that makes the journey through change magical (okay, or maybe just packed with way more opportunities for self-trust instead of self-doubt or criticism).

Here's why: When you approach what you do or don't know with curiosity, you are focusing on learning through living rather than simply achieving the goal. Yes, you want something for yourself, but by embracing curiosity, you'll learn that there isn't only one way to get there.

There is not just one way to live your life. There are in fact infinite ways if you are willing to stay curious. Curiosity is not simply a desire to know or learn something. It is a life-changing tool that allows you to open your mind to all the options available to you.

The shift that you have to make is from a mindset focused on certainty to one focused on curiosity.

It's about asking yourself "What if?" instead of "How exactly?" The "what if" question is more open-ended and will be mind-expanding. It allows for your thoughts and dreams and plans to develop naturally. It is important because while you cultivate, water, and weed through your shifting soil, it's not about having all the answers. It's about trusting the want in your heart, allowing yourself space to play with options for actions, and gaining confidence along the way. It's also about prioritizing yourself and giving yourself time to get curious about how you can grow.

The real work in this phase is to *stay* curious. Stay as kind, open, and real with yourself as you can. This is a place to be honest, creative, and brave with yourself. Allow yourself to think with freedom and grace when it comes to any shifting soil you might be processing. There is not only one way to make change for the better. Stay curious so that you can see your options and decide which is best for you at that moment.

Tool for Practice

EXPLORE THE RUB

As you endure (and eventually, embrace) the Shifting Soil phase of the Growth Cycle, the goal is to give those feelings time and space, but also remember that you have options for change if you can choose to stay curious.

I've included several reflection questions to help you explore where you might have shifting soil in your heart and soul. As you think on the questions below, feel free to use the work you've already done. Go back and revisit your Seeker Statement, Dream Day Exercise, or your Personal Manifesto. Now is the time to do that with a bit more curiosity. Reread your responses to those three Tools for Practice, then ask yourself these questions:

* Where in my life am in not in alignment with what I say I want?

* Where might I have some level of discomfort, dissatisfaction, or frustration in my life that I need to slow down and listen to?

* What does the shifting soil in my life feel like? What are some strategies I might employ to manage any discomfort that might arise?

* What are several options to consider as I try to grow toward what I want?

Don't ignore the gift being presented by Shifting Soil. This is a chance to listen to yourself, trust that it has something to say, that a change for the better is possible and available to you, one that your heart and soul want. This phase won't always be pleasant, there will definitely be growing pains to manage, but the rub will be worth it as you learn how to love yourself through the learning process. Remember: You know more than you think you know, and curiosity is the key.

In the next phase of the Growth Cycle—Breaking Through—you'll have the chance to use your Seeker's everyday bravery as you choose to break through and truly explore new territory in your growth.

SHIFTING SOIL

ROOTING TRUST

THE *Growth* CYCLE

BREAKING THROUGH

PACING PURSUIT

Chapter 6

GROWTH CYCLE PHASE 2
BREAKING THROUGH

In the first phase of the Growth Cycle—Shifting Soil—the truth to let soak in is this: Change is always happening around you. It is inevitable, and there is nothing you (or anyone else) can do to stop it. But you have the choice to become more aware of the shifting soil in your soul and to learn from what it is telling you. When your heart, soul, gut, body, or intuition experience a longing for change and you feel the rub, the best way to keep growing is to slow down and give yourself time to acknowledge it, feel it, and then choose to get curious about options available to you.

Awareness is only the first step, though. Much of that first phase of the Growth Cycle helps you shine a light not only on the desire but also on the opportunities you have to grow out of a situation where you no longer feel firmly rooted. Still, allowing curiosity to help you identify options for action is drastically different than actually trying and taking action. You can become aware of something, give it some of your mental focus, but still choose to do nothing about it. It happens to everyone at some point. Why we choose to stay in shifting soil that is uncomfortable and sometimes downright painful, stifling our personal growth, is slightly different for everyone—but the choices begging to be made are the same.

Will you choose to stay stuck and settle for less than you deserve?
Will you choose to allow the opportunity to grow to finally outweigh your fear of the unknown?
Will you prioritize yourself and pursue your potential?
Will you break through into something new?

That's what this book is all about—seeking growth through change. You've learned so much already, and the Seeker in me is certain that you are ready to honor the Seeker in you. So, let's dig into the second phase of the Growth Cycle—Breaking Through—so that you can learn how to keep growing and move from awareness to action.

What Is Breaking Through

Breaking Through is a pivotal phase in the Growth Cycle because it's your soul's cry for a decision. Your soul is asking *will we stay stuck or will we grow?* Although we all have to pass through the Shifting Soil phase, you don't want to get stuck there. Lingering in shifting soil where you feel you want to change, yet you haven't committed to going for it, leaves you in a state of limbo and unease.

You need to move through your shifting soil so that you can reach the next phase. In Breaking Through, you find yourself at an inflection point—a true tipping point—where you finally put your hands to the plow, make the decision to act, and try something (anything) to grow forward. You choose to believe that you can survive new things to live and learn *through action.*

Deep in my heart I hope you choose to try one of the many options available to you by harnessing everyday bravery. You can't know unless you try—and Breaking Through is where you go for it.

Let me keep it real, though: When you commit to start breaking through, it can (and very likely will) get uncomfortable. Naturally, this period is one of potential disruption—okay, guaranteed disruption—but the level of intensity will vary. You are choosing to take action, but that doesn't mean you won't get dirty as you dig new paths forward.

What Breaking Through Looks and Feels Like

You and I can agree that change for the better is an opportunity to grow. But I think we can also agree that we will delay change time and time again because of the possible discomfort of said change. And here's a sentence you might have said that keeps you safely in the soul-sucking status quo…

It's not that bad.

I know those words because I've said them myself. I've had Shifting Soil seasons in my life that I held at bay for years because it simply wasn't that bad. Or maybe more adequately put, the pain of staying put didn't yet outweigh the pain of committing to action.

I use the word *pain* broadly, so that it can include all sorts of pain: actual physical pain, since I am a believer that the body tells you when it is not happy; emotional or psychological pain; or an intellectual disconnect from where you are and where you think can be. Whichever way you feel it, let me guarantee you the following:

There will come a time when you finally feel *compelled* to change. When you can no longer pretend that it's fine, you're fine, everything is fine. It's not fine anymore. It *is* that bad.

That compulsion to commit to change for the better is a beautiful, freeing moment where you decide that the risk of the unknown is not as great as the cost of inaction. That conviction is breaking through!

So, how do you actually reach toward positive change, growth, and optimism, and reject staying stuck? It's not what anyone would call *easy*, but it might help to recall these truths:

- You are safe.
- You are a leader.
- You know more than you think you know.
- You are your own best guide.

Breakthrough moments are meant to serve you, to alleviate the pain and suffering you're currently experiencing. Luckily, not all changes are from rocky and turbulent situations. In fact, some of the harder changes to make are ones where the life you currently live makes sense from the outside looking in.

For example, you might have a solid career, good pay, and decent or above-average benefits. You might have a family you care about and who appreciate you, a team you love, clients that pay well, and managers that truly value you. You might be able to afford all the material things you want and need. But maybe even with all that, something has been (or is still) missing. The spark of life. The person you used to feel like. The joy and energy and enthusiasm you once had. The impact you long to share in your community. You have explored the Shifting Soil, and you know that even though others might think your life looks great, it's time to take action and make a change for the better.

I understand that state all too well.

On February 2, 2018, I walked out the doors of an award-winning, highly respected, Austin, Texas-based accounting firm that I called home for the last seven years of my corporate career. I'd climbed up the corporate ladder and was perched on a top rung serving alongside other partners, managing the nonprofit practice filled with talented people and mission-driven work.

But I decided to leave.

Why? Was it awful there? Did you have a bad experience, Dena?

Nope. Quite the opposite. It was wonderful.

I consider myself lucky to have spent time within the walls of a firm that proved time and time again that they mean what they say on their website: We care for our people.

They weren't lying. The firm's culture consistently lived out its core values, including my favorite that no success at work is worth failure at home.

But if this firm was so great, then why would I leave? Why did I sit down with the managing partner and share my heart's desire to explore a new path for myself and then spend nearly three years preparing to walk away? Why would I turn my back on a path that included a six-figure salary, benefits, insurance for my family, and a team of rockstar peers and clients that made me smile every day? Why would I choose to venture down the entrepreneurial path where I had no real clue what to do except fake it until I could hopefully make it?

The answer was simple. I finally decided that *I* was worth the risk.

I'd been aware for years (if you do the math, I knew for like 12 years, yikes!) that I was in shifting soil when it came to my chosen profession. My career wasn't *that* bad. I enjoyed the people side of things, made good money, had great benefits, but when I went home I didn't feel anything but a dull ache that something was missing. I couldn't imagine doing it for the long haul. After making partner, I felt reenergized in that new role for about a year, but I again started to stare at the picture on my office wall—*Don't quit your day dreams*. I finally trusted my gut and knew that I was ready to break through and commit to action.

I decided that no success at work was worth a failure in my home. It just happened that although my home life looked great from the outside, there was turmoil there. My marriage needed serious attention. My personal obligations and my professional aspirations needed tending at the same time. And while my work wasn't a contributing factor to my marriage's unhealthiness, it was a huge part of my identity and how I experienced my life. And the truth was that I was finally ready to honor my shifting soil and break through. I didn't want to fail myself any longer. Just like the saying *home is where the heart is*, I had to honor my soul's calling that I had other important work to do.

I decided that I couldn't live my life by other's standards. I decided that the risk of looking back with regret was far worse than the risk of failure.

I bet on myself and my dreams and took a leap of faith, trusting that everything would somehow be okay. And it was none other than the firm's managing partner that helped me cement all those decisions and gave me the peace of mind I needed to continue on my journey.

In my debut memoir, *Road to Hope*, I shared how my managing partner Steve (who always looked a bit like my dad to me) patiently waited for a break in my nervous chatter as I shared my dreams and possible plans to leave. We were sitting across from each other on a sunny afternoon at a high-top table at a restaurant just blocks away from the office. With two glasses of iced tea sweating in between us, mirroring my own nervous perspiration, he finally got his chance to speak, and said,

"Dena. Everything is going to be okay. Want to know how I know?"
I nodded and waited with curious anticipation.
"Because you are smiling."

I was smiling. I had done it. I had trusted myself and the process of life. I still couldn't see exactly where I was headed, but I'd been brave enough to control what I could control: myself and my choices. I hadn't lost all fear, but I'd decided I could and would grow in spite of them.

Fearless growth (my chosen mantra at the time) meant that I'd get to know my fears better and on purpose. Then I'd ask my fears to remain with me as we continued to move forward. We—me and my fears—we could be safe. We could grow together.

You've Got Choices to Make

Life is about choices. And most of those choices (luckily) are not life or death. The choice in front of you now is if you'll finally move from thinking to doing. You have practiced slowing down and getting curious. You have asked yourself what you want in your Inspired Life. You've given yourself time to imagine your Dream Day, create a Personal Manifesto. But to move from Shifting Soil into Breaking Through, you have to honor any fear you still might have and choose to dig even deeper to find the courage to grow, actively choose to break out of old patterns or ruts, and break through to new paths and possibilities.

The Breaking Through phase might feel like a moment that comes and goes, or you might linger in it before making an ultimate decision. Some breakthrough decisions will smack you in the face, and you'll have this huge moment where you clearly see you have a choice to make and that the time to act on it is now. Some will creep up on you and try to hide in sheep's clothing. There's no one path to get there. But I guarantee that there will come a point where you'll look yourself in the eye and know that your soul is getting tired of the shifting soil and is ready for an answer to this question:

Are we staying or growing?

I have already talked about how I made this choice in my professional life. But I also needed to think about breaking through in my personal life.

At that time, my marriage had been waning for several years. We married so young and did our best to figure out how to be husband and wife. We had to figure out how to start careers, pay bills, and become actual adults. Then, for a matter of years after our babies joined the family and our responsibilities grew, we didn't know how to slow down and focus on ourselves or our marriage. It was simply not getting the attention it deserved. We were both doing the best we could with the tools that we had at the time, but they weren't enough.

For years, I'd been mired in the shifting soil as a farmer's wife where his time and priorities drifted to the farm and away from us. I felt slighted, I felt angry, and mostly, I felt alone. My soul knew we needed to make a change, knew that we needed to take action to create a breakthrough of any kind, but I was too scared of what it would be like to talk to him about any of it. My childhood up-bringing had trained me all too well to avoid conflict.

So, for many years, when I'd get rubbed the wrong way, I chose to harbor resentment rather than honor the longing of my soul to take action and find a way toward a healthier, happier marriage. As the years wore on, my soul wore down. I began to feel so lonely and isolated, and for those who know, there is nothing worse than feeling lonely inside a marriage or relationship. But even in my despair, I chose to do nothing, and that was the mistake. Action was going to be the only way to begin a breakthrough. A conversation. A letter. A text. Any way of sharing my truth with him would have been the better choice to make than staying silent.

It always feels so counterintuitive to me that the person you have shared some of the most personal and intimate moments of your life with is often the same person you can't seem to bring yourself to share your deep, real, authentic truth. I had been through so much with JP, why was it so hard for me to tell him what I truly wanted? But since we had never created a shared vision for our shared Inspired Lives, we were flying blind, going through marriage on autopilot, doing what seemed to make sense each day. At the same time, we were failing to do the things that really mattered. We weren't slowing ourselves down enough to dream together, to choose to be Seekers together, and to make collective *US*-Turns back in toward ourselves as a couple.

In hindsight, I had numerous opportunities to break through in my marriage, multiple chances to use a YOU-Turn by sharing my sh!t or asking for help with our relationship. The simple yet sad fact is that I simply wasn't equipped or ready to use them, let alone take action. So, the discomfort of the shifting soil kept building in intensity. Each time I ignored myself, I was also missing out on another chance to move on to the next phase of the Growth Cycle.

I went on that way for years, until one day, I was finally ready to break through. To be honest, when I felt this pull to act, I thought it would be the beginning of our end. I'd been hearing whispers in my mind saying *separate*. And with a stubborn sense of resignation, I knew I had no choice but to venture into unfamiliar and unsteadying conversations with my husband because the risk of pretending that our marriage was healthy was no longer worth it to me.

I wish I could share that there was a magical, easy-to-spot *aha!* moment, but there wasn't. There was an internal reckoning that knew I would not settle until I did something. Something other than seeking refuge outside my own home. A part of me knew that I wanted, needed, and deserved more from a marriage. That's why I chose to break through my fear and asked him to meet me on the couch as I shakily asked and answered questions we both needed answers to.

As we talked that night and I revealed to him the depths of my unhappiness and admitted my emotional affair, I knew I was already veering into unsafe territory. I could feel us both losing hope, leaning into despair, choosing to let our marriage die. I'm not going to lie—it was a close call. I had moments where I thought we wouldn't make it, both that night and as well as for some time afterward. But we chose to keep growing, and we agreed to do all of it without any guarantee of the result (there never is a guarantee, I'm sorry to confirm). Neither of us had any idea if our marriage would survive.

Then one morning, as I shared my sad, ugly real-life sh!t with Alisa, one of my dearest friends (and who I'll forever credit for saving my marriage), she said to me, "What if you are supposed to separate from someone other than JP?" Her kind, open, and real curiosity was a lightning rod to my soul. Her question gave me an entirely new perspective on the breakthrough I was growing through.

The wheels in my head started to spin in a different direction. And in that moment, I knew she was right. I did not want to separate from JP. I wanted to try. I decided to try and see my husband for who he was—a man, doing the best he could, with the tools he had then. A man who loved me and believed in us. So, together, we decided we were willing to be Seekers together and chose to try, which is a brave thing to do. And I'm proud to share that we both would say that our marriage is the best it's ever been. Both of us have experienced so much growth together and on our own. We are absolutely still learning, but we've both gotten more comfortable with choosing action sooner rather than later. If we feel off, we choose not to ignore it, but rather have the awkward conversation and see where it leads us.

Let me be honest: Choosing to break through wasn't easy. While it was exciting and new to think all day about the options, the endless possibilities, the risks, and the rewards. What ultimately proved to make my hope for positive change in my life become my reality was ACTION. And it will be the same for you.

It is vital that you honor the hopes you have in your heart through action. Hope alone is merely wishful thinking. But hope partnered with action? Now that's living and learning along the ever-winding way, making choice after intentional choice, fueled by your discerning gut. It's the way to truly live the dream... your Inspired Life!

The decision you'll be faced with over and over again during this phase of the Growth Cycle is simple: Stay stuck or grow forward?

Then, once you make the choice that I trust you will (to keep growing), it's time to go one step further and truly commit to the pursuit of your potential. But as you do that, please keep in mind a few things: You can only control what you can control, and throughout it all you must care for yourself.

Care for Yourself

As the Breaking Through phase progresses, it can bring about quite a shock to your system. Circumstances in your life are giving you a reason to pause and think about the choices at hand. Your mind might be in constant motion, thinking about why you should or shouldn't make the change. And it's in those times that we grow weary. That's when we might choose to stay stuck or make rash decisions that don't serve us.

You will find that one or all of the YOU-Turns will support you through this phase as well—trust that you matter, listen to your voice, ask for help, share your stuff, or explore more. The YOU-Turns start to weave into your Seeker way of living and growing, and for this phase specifically, you will find that the changes you choose to pursue will help you build a stronger, deeper level of self-trust.

I can't guarantee you that growth will be without discomfort. Actually, it's likely quite the opposite. By choosing to be a Seeker, choosing to try and create your Inspired Life, growing pains are inevitable. Sometimes the emotional exposure will be high, and other times it might feel like a blip on the radar. Regardless, it's vital that as you break through you care for yourself as best you can—by slowing down and getting a grip on yourself, your feelings, and the stories you are telling yourself—to help you regulate the mental, physical, and emotional experience of this phase of the Growth Cycle. And here's a way to help you do just that.

Get a G.R.I.P.

How many times have you said to yourself or told someone else that they just need to get a grip? Getting a grip is a call to snap out of an emotionally charged and maybe sometimes irrational state, the ability to regain your composure, to self-regulate your emotional reaction to any situation you might find yourself in.

I'd like to add to that idea. Let me break down what I mean by G.R.I.P. *G* means to give your feelings time and space, *R* means to regulate your breathing, *I* means to imagine other options, and *P* means to pace yourself. Once you better understand how to get a G.R.I.P. you can practice working through it now or the very next time you feel a breakthrough is imminent—actually, when any phase of the Growth Cycle feels overwhelming.

G = *Give your feelings time and space.* In sisters Emily and Amelia Nagoski's book *Burnout* they speak to the importance of completing the stress cycle. They assert that *dealing with your stress* is a separate process (the stress cycle) from dealing with *the things that cause your stress* (the stressors). They teach women that we must be able to understand the differences between *stressors*— things that activate the stress response in our body, such as external stressors that our brain and body believe can bring us harm—and *stress*—the neurological and physiological shift that happens when our bodies encounter those threats.

Our bodies need a cue that we are safe, and unfortunately, the sisters' research shows that women get stuck in what they call "the tunnel." We are activated by a stressor and our body dives into a tunnel, but instead of taking the time to work its way out the other side, we remove or numb the stressors. We assume or even believe that we should be stress-free. But when we react that way, we're simply stuck in the middle of the tunnel. By not completing the stress cycle time and time again, women experience chronic stress and life-threatening illness.

They explain that on average physical and emotional responses to stressors last 30-90 seconds, but we're so quick to try to shut them down because they make us uncomfortable. Instead of allowing us to feel those emotions for a minute or so and then move on, we stay stuck in them! They keep us in the middle of the tunnel, unable to reach the light at the end.

The trick, they argue, is to try to give your feelings time and space to have their say. The next time your stomach sinks, or heat rises in your cheeks, or your hands tingle, I encourage you to stop what you are doing, close your eyes, and simply allow yourself to feel the sensations. You can try and count up from zero until they pass. Literally give them time to work through your system. Respect your feelings, and they will respect you.

R = *Regulate your breathing.* As you encounter peaks of stress, remind yourself to stop and breathe. When was the last time you stopped and took a long deep breath? Can't remember? Well, that simply won't do. In times of stress or just in our hustle and bustle, busy-bee life, we fall prey to shallow breathing. And when we do that, our bodies aren't getting what they need, which can lead to fatigue and muscle tension. As you journey through your Growth Cycle, one of the easiest (and completely free!) tricks is to stop and take a breath.

I invite you now to close your eyes, get comfortable, and take three deep breaths. You might even try "box breathing." In this four-step breathing technique, you breathe in, filling up those lungs to the count of four, then hold your breath for four seconds, then slowly exhale for four seconds, then hold for another four, and then of course, exhale. Repeat this cycle until you feel "chill." Another fantastic technique is the 4x6 breathing, where you inhale for four beats and then exhale for six. The longer exhale does something magical and is absolutely worth a shot. Breathing intentionally like that is a proven way to reduce stress, increase calm, lower blood pressure and heart rate, reduce muscle tension, and relieve anxiety. It will help you focus on what you need to do!

And if you find that you are working through a stressful period of change or transition, grab another sticky note, jot down "Just Breathe!" and stick it in a place you'll see it frequently. Or text a friend and ask them to remind you to breathe every once in a while. It never hurts to have a friend on your side, helping you care for yourself and your growth!

There is also a whole community of passionate people and professionals that specialize in breath work. Go online and check it out if you feel so moved. Or you can attend a local meditation session or a yoga class, or just practice your breathing while sitting in traffic. There are so many ways you can easily fit in more of the life-giving oxygen you need and deserve.

I = *Imagine other options, possibilities, or endings.* As you enter and move through the Breaking Through phase, you'll move from awareness to a more active form of growth, and with that we begin to think of all the what ifs that might come from the changes we're pursuing. Remember that our brain wants to keep us safe, but sometimes it will weave multiple false narratives of what could happen. One of fear's tools is to conjure up all the worst-case scenarios that could spring up and negatively impact you. But as you are becoming more and more comfortable playing in the space of possibility, you can also practice imagining other, more positive options. What if it turns out exactly like you had hoped? What if it turns out better? After giving your feelings time and space and taking several deep breaths, use your humble curiosity to imagine several possible positive (dare I say, happy) endings.

This is also a time to practice assuming the best in yourself and others. So what if you take action and things don't go exactly as planned? Trust that you did the best you could with the tools you had in that moment. Try assuming that anyone you might have to engage with in complex, complicated, emotionally infused conversations truly wants the best for you and was also doing the best they could with the tools they had in that moment. When we imagine other options, possibilities, or endings, we expand the endless ways that our breakthrough can play out in real life.

With any breakthrough, the goal is to have a healthy, emotionally regulated, positive, and proactive encounter with yourself and others. So, don't allow yourself to get stuck assuming the worst, anticipating the worst, fearing the worst. Fear will do nothing but ramp up your fight or flight responses, upping the cortisol in your blood. Instead, imagine other options, possibilities, and endings. Play in the beautiful land of everything going right.

Next time, before entering a new interaction with someone, ask yourself, "how do I want to walk out of this feeling?" If you focus on what you want—feeling like you were honest, that you were heard, that you were kind, and felt kindness in return—just see what happens. *You will always find what you go looking for.* So, as you break through, choose to give yourself permission to imagine other, more inspiring and empowering ways things can keep growing.

P = *Pace yourself, a.k.a., pause and circle back.* We will talk more specifically about pacing when we get to the third phase of the Growth Cycle—Pacing Pursuit. But for now, as you focus on breaking through, here's a new way you can focus on pacing: Pause and circle back. If you feel that you are losing control, tell yourself you are going to push pause, give yourself some distance from the situation. Then when it feels right, circle back with yourself. If you are in a conversation with someone and you need to pause, simply tell them that you'd like a moment to regain your composure. Offer up an amount of time before you'd like to circle back and reengage in the conversation. Yes, it will feel odd the first time you do it with yourself or others, but you'll get better at it.

In any situation, if you don't have all the answers and it's freaking you out, pause and circle back. If you are at a breaking point and your temper is threatening to burn you or others, pause and circle back. If you are worried your boss, mom, dad, sister, friend, husband/wife/partner is not going to take news of your change well, pause and circle back.

In each pause, go back through the three previous steps (*G, R, I*) and work to regain your emotional footing and composure. Then decide the best approach to circle back to the topic and possible breakthrough at hand. Options might include time for self-reflection, a walk, journaling, or sharing what feels right with trusted people in your life. Whatever you decide, pace yourself and choose to slow down rather than speed up. Pause and circle back as you find ways to get a well-deserved G.R.I.P. Those steps are truly one of the best ways to care for yourself in this phase.

Tool for Practice

Forget-me-nots, beautiful bundles of little blue flowers, symbolize true love and respect. But when it comes to the breakthrough, the biggest thing in the way of growth is avoidance. To honor the spirit of the forget-me-nots, though, and to show yourself some mad love and respect, I'm inviting you to stop and think about choices for action that you are avoiding in this Avoid-Me-Not Tool for Practice.

And now that you know how to chill yourself out, remember that this phase of the Growth Cycle is really all about choices—to stay in the shifting soil or to take action and break through and care for yourself as best you can. Let's relinquish the idea that there are good or bad, right or wrong choices. Now, I know there are moral compasses that we all must honor, but for the sake of growth, this phase is simply begging you to make a choice. There is no one right way to grow.

So, allow these questions to help you reflect on the actions you could be making for yourself right now, the ones you are avoiding, and the risks that are weighing on you as you work to decide whether you will break through:

* Is there any shifting soil in my soul that is calling (more loudly than others) for a decision to act?

* What does that action look like (e.g., a conversation with someone, applying for something, letting something/someone go)?

* What am I most fearful could happen if I choose to commit to take action and explore the options available to me?

* What could be possible in my life if I chose to commit to action and grow toward a change for the better?

If by your answers you feel yourself physically respond to things that you are avoiding, stop and actively get a G.R.I.P. That in itself will help you get more comfortable with the emotional response of breaking through and will be a tool that will serve you time and time again.

Committing to take action toward positive change requires every-day bravery. The changes you want to make for yourself can and most likely will impact others in your life, and learning how to navigate the Breaking Through phase when other people are involved requires the choice to prioritize yourself and use those trusty YOU-Turns. It's not easy work, but it isn't supposed to be. Now, however, you have new tools. You can take action *and* get a G.R.I.P. to stay grounded in a place of calm and care as you Break Through.

Once you start taking action, the next phase of the Growth Cycle—Pacing Pursuit—is all about learning how to safely grow at your own pace. Let's keep growing!

SHIFTING SOIL

ROOTING TRUST

THE *Growth* CYCLE

BREAKING THROUGH

PACING PURSUIT

Chapter 7

GROWTH CYCLE PHASE 3
PACING PURSUIT

When I was in middle school, I began to have headaches. I struggled to see things. My parents took me to the eye doctor for testing, which showed that I needed glasses. I chose my frames and was fitted for my new four-eyed adventure. I don't remember what they looked like, but I do remember that on my way home, I stared out the window at the leaves on the trees. After not seeing them clearly for years, I was fascinated by how beautiful they were. With my vision corrected, I could now see each individual leaf fluttering in the breeze. I saw how the sunlight hit each part of the tree differently. Now that I could see perfectly again, my life was suddenly so much more beautiful—and so much more complex.

I remembered that awakening in my physical vision when, almost 20 years later, I experienced what I called my soul awakening. At what I would call a rock bottom—my marriage nearly imploding alongside the terrifying potential of leaving behind my professional career and the safety and security it afforded—I decided that I could actually figure out how to change for the better. I felt like I was given new eyes. I woke up from the unconscious, unintentional, and unfulfilling ways I was seeing my life. I decided to pursue what I believed was my potential—a slightly unclear, yet distinctly better version of me, my work, and my marriage that I knew I could work toward.

That's exactly what I hope has happened with you as you've been reading this book and doing the Tools for Practice. I hope that you too are "seeing" in a whole new way. You have chosen to be a Seeker and have the vision for your Inspired Life in your mind's eye. You have new tools helping you make frequent YOU-Turns as you grow. And with those turns back into yourself, you've learned you must trust yourself to grow forward through the Growth Cycle.

You have done amazing work. And, if it hasn't dawned on you yet to be really freaking proud of yourself—this is your cue to stop, take a deep breath, and celebrate yourself for growing this far! We'll learn more about the power of praising yourself soon in the *Harvest* section, but after giving yourself a few internal high fives, keep reading. You still have some things to learn to complete the Growth Cycle, so let's move into Pacing Pursuit.

What Is Pacing Pursuit

Just like a plant that finally battles its way through the earth and starts raising its head toward the sun, your soul will want to seek the warmth of light and love as soon as it breaks through. Once your soul gets a taste of growth, it will want more. It will want to find and feel more freedom, to experience more of the exhilaration that can come from curiosity-led choice and authentic action. You will feel passionate and purposeful about your life. Your heart and soul will feel alive and want to bask in the glory as they grow—and they won't want to lose that feeling.

It is a wonderful, positive, and exciting process, but it's not meant to all happen at once. Growth is most productive when it happens naturally over time. When seedlings or sprouts first emerge from the ground, their job is simple—find water and sun. And sometimes, they will charge toward the sun and sadly get burned. Or if they have too much of what they are looking for, stalks can grow all too quickly leaving them weak and at risk of snapping with a gust of wind. It's the same for us. If we grow too much too fast, we can get hurt. If we focus on fast growth, or throw all caution to the wind, we might unintentionally jeopardize the sustained growth we're longing for in our Inspired Life. That's why in this phase of the Growth Cycle, we want to learn how we can safely grow at our own unique pace.

What Pacing Pursuit Looks and Feels Like

Looking back, when I was first in this phase of the Growth Cycle, I moved too quickly and got burned. I rushed toward new people and new ideas with wild abandon. I lost track of my own need to grow slowly, to truly digest what I was living and learning, and garner my own meaning out of what I was growing through. I simply clung to what other people were saying or doing, nodding in agreement and feeling like their way must be *the* way.

I'd go all-in on the ideologies of experts in the personal growth and self-help industry, but I didn't really have a working understanding of it in my own life. I was spewing mantras and things from books and podcasts I was consuming, thinking I could just grow quickly by intellectual osmosis. Seeking new information is not a bad thing, of course. Quite the opposite, it's fantastic. I simply couldn't contain my excitement! I wanted to grow as much as I could as quickly as I could, but I didn't know how to pace myself or really think for myself—how this new information applied to *me* in *my* life.

In chasing movement forward at all-out speeds, your soul simply can't keep up. It's like going to the gym, pumping the iron that you haven't touched in months (or years, or never), and then being so sore that you can't move the next day. What typically happens is that you conclude that you must not be meant to lift weights and then never step foot back in that place again. Your excitement got the best of you, but your lack of patience in the process got you in the end.

To avoid all-too-soon halts to growth, you have to learn to monitor your intensity and pacing. That tempo is our work now in the Growth Cycle. The Pacing Pursuit phase is about finding and creating safe and simple steps forward that will support your growth to create a long-term, sustainable path forward. Yes, you've got an Inspired Life to create, but the way to get there is not by rushing yourself, risking it all, and potentially harming yourself and others in the process. Instead, I'm encouraging you to harness one of the Seeker's superpowers—disciplined consistency—as you focus on keeping things safe and simple and pacing yourself.

Keep It Safe and Simple

In order to create the Inspired Life you want, you'll need to move forward one step at a time. Right foot, left foot, right foot, left foot. That focus means choosing to live with a down-and-dirty level of disciplined consistency. It doesn't mean that you push aside confidence, passion, or drive. What it means is that you must choose to take small, meaningful steps forward over and over again to grow strong and healthy dreams. That's how you'll keep growing safely.

How can you decide what is a safe, small, meaningful step? Well, it's as simple as thinking about all the options you have available and committing to one, at least to start. But before diving in, you ask yourself this question—*Is that simple enough?*

Choose a possible action you could take now to get you one step closer to your Inspired Life, and sit with that question for a moment. *Is it simple enough?* If it feels overwhelming, maybe a bit too much to tackle, then make it smaller! Break down your next change-seeking action even further so that your next steps will be safe and simple but still keep you moving forward.

And even if taking those safe and simple steps forward leaves you needing to get a G.R.I.P. (like we just learned about), that's okay. The goal is that we slow ourselves down and stop racing toward our growth with wild abandon. Instead, like plants, we should seek sun and water with a growing sense of peace and discernment that comes from keeping things safe and simple.

Your goal now is to keep things growing. Once you start to take simple steps forward that you feel comfortable with, *then* you can always begin to scale up the complexity. If you stop trying to rush your growth, and instead move with purpose and thoughtfulness, then over time, when you are ready, the safe and simple approach will increase the scale of your efforts naturally. You will organically scale up to building new habits, instilling new patterns of thinking and behaving, and in the end trusting your natural momentum and intuition.

This way of scaling up what is safe and simple to *you* is a means to the desired end. It shows that you are learning how to keep growing day in and day out. Does that approach take more time to learn and grow rather than jumping in all at once? *Sure, maybe.*

Can it be frustrating to feel like you aren't growing or achieving as fast or as big as someone else? *Sure, again.*

But only you can know what feels right for you. And if you really want to make a change for the better, then trust that choosing to keep growing in ways that feel safe and simple is worth a shot.

Whatever it is that you truly want as you maneuver through the Pacing Pursuit phase, it's the perfect time to *slow down* and hone in on the speed at which you pursue growth.

Pace Yourself

Pacing is necessary for navigating change because it is a very personal practice. No one grows at the exact same speed. No one can know for anyone else what they can and cannot sustain when it comes to personal growth. No one can rush themselves or anyone else into a change for the better.

That's why we have to focus on the speed at which we grow up, out, and forward. We don't want to risk an all too speedy start that leads us to a full face-plant from mental and emotional exhaustion. You can only grow as fast as your soul will allow.

Let me try to explain it this way. Your life journey is not necessarily a race, but to help illustrate my point, let me share a personal experience that helped me better understand the importance of pacing myself. On your mark, get set, go…

Insert the image of a whistle, a road, and some gym shoes into the scenario there and please know that my stomach would drop.

I do not consider myself a runner... never have and most likely never will. I have run before and will probably run again, but it's not a physical activity that has ever come easy to me.

With a shaking head and terribly uncomfortable feelings, I can remember running a timed mile in elementary school. I remember the sweat, my cheeks feeling like they were on fire. I remember feeling so slow, wishing my sports bra was a bit more comfortable, but mostly, the painful burn in my lungs. I could not catch my breath. I shuffled my way to the finish line. I didn't die. But I decided then and there that I was not a fan of running. I didn't like feeling slow in comparison to all the other kids. And I really didn't like the fact that I simply could not breathe as I panted and wheezed to gulp in air.

No one had taught me the lesson that if your lungs get tired before your legs, you're running too fast! Maybe if I'd known, I could have slowed myself down, managed my breathing, and found a pace that fit me just right. But I had no such luck.

Allow a solid 30 years to pass and at the ripe age of 41, I decided I wanted to run a 5k (darn Shifting Soil moments). And not just finish the race, but actually *run* the whole darn thing. I'd finished races before, but I walked/jogged/slogged my way through them. In my heart this time, however, I wanted to *RUN* the race of just over 3 miles all the way through.

Pretty quickly, I knew what I had to do. I had to phone a friend. I reached out to my runner friend, Kim, and told her I'd love her help. I was clear in what my goal was and trusted that she'd teach me ways to make it happen. Of particular note here is that I made a YOU-Turn and asked for help, knowing it was an important part of my growth. (Yes, I *do* practice what I preach!)

Kim was the person I reached out to because she is a runner.

Like a *real* runner. She's a runner who chose to do cross-country in high school and get up early on weekends to run... *what?* And then as an adult, Kim would choose to run halfway across our really big state for fun... *what?* Flip over to me who again for most of my life would shout to the world, "I am not a runner. I cannot run."

But that year, I had some shifting soil begging to be tended, and I wanted to run that race. I knew that when it came to my stamina or speed, maybe I couldn't run as far as others or as fast as many, but I also decided that it didn't matter what others could do. I wanted to see what *I* could do. I wanted to see if I could in fact run the entire way from the starting line to the finish line.

Kim was gracious when I asked for her help. She ran with me and taught me the importance of pacing. She taught me that running too fast or too slow could keep me from reaching my goals because I'd run out of energy before I reached the end of the course. She explained that in previous races where I'd started off running but ended up walking, I was most likely running too fast, too soon, which exhausted me prematurely. She explained the importance of pacing myself. She said pacing was about finding the consistent, safe, and steady speed that would keep me moving forward.

Kim helped me put pacing into practice when we trained together. She had us run at a pace that she felt I could manage (which was much slower than her standard pace, I might add). But she ran right in front of me to give me focus. She was my pace-setting human inspiration.

Then, race day came and good things happened. I ran the whole race. Kim stuck by my side the entire time, taking a selfie for proof (and of course an IG post later). And I was so proud of myself. Kim had taught me that I had to learn and respect what pace worked best in my endeavor.

And it's no different when we're trying to keep growing. You have to find a pace that works for you. Just like races acknowledge and have different starting positions for people with different mile pacings (meaning slower people to the back... ahem, that's me) we must acknowledge that people grow at different speeds as well. So, if you feel your lungs giving out before your legs, slow down to go at your pace. Let time take time (more on that nugget of wisdom in Chapter 10).

Trust When It's Time to Adjust Your Pacing

I'd say for the pacing of this chapter, I should speed it up and get on to the next point. But allow me to share just a bit more of my running adventure with Kim, because it really illustrates what we're getting at here in Pacing Pursuit. Just over a year and a half after that first running goal, I reached out to Kim again because, darn it, I had another shift in my soul's soil (cue another time through the Growth Cycle for me, yippee!). And this time it was saying *Dena, you can run faster.*

I chose to commit to action. Cue Kim coming in like the rockstar runner and amazing friend she is after I sent her a text telling her that I wanted to ramp up my pace. She responded quickly and coached me toward my dream of shaving nearly a minute off a previously timed one-mile run. Of course, it was not going to be easy, but again, she helped me create a plan to safely ramp up my pacing. It took a series of simple upticks in intensity.

Days later I went to the gym, hopped on the treadmill, and set a personal record on a mile run. But I left feeling I could have gone farther, faster. My soul was ready for more of a challenge.

So, I chose to challenge myself and adjust my pacing again to try and shave off even more time, to try and believe in myself like Kim believed in me. I shared my stuff with her, telling her I wanted to try and go even faster. Here's all I will say: Find friends like Kim. Friends who believe you can and should challenge yourself. Friends who text you back and give you confidence, telling you, "Go for it and report back."

Find friends who push you, believe in you, and are waiting for you to REPORT BACK. There is so much power in having someone believe in you, but also having someone hold you accountable for going out and doing what you say you want to do—that's a growth game changer. If you can make the YOU-Turn of *asking for help* and find friends who will be a guide and gauge as you test out different paces, good things will happen—things that make you proud of yourself and super grateful for the gift of friendship.

So, remember: Pace yourself and trust when something in you says to adjust your pacing. Whatever dream you're chasing, whatever part of your Inspired Life you are pursuing, pace yourself. If you can manage your breathing and keep taking solid, consistent steps forward, you might have found the right pacing for you. If you feel the need for speed, honor that urge and try to increase your pace. If you feel like you can't catch your breath—physically or emotionally—slow down. And if you simply can't keep going, stop, then reassess your situation and create a new plan for action.

When it comes to pacing ourselves, I see two options that are available:

- *Speed up*
- *Slow down*

Many times, we want to speed ourselves up, but let me be clear on this—it's okay to slow your roll in the name of growth. Whether it's your life pacing, the speed at which you make decisions, or the rhythm by which you operate, there is zero shame in a slow-moving train.

Be that little engine that could. Repeat, *I think I can, I think I can.* Growing at a pace that you or others might deem too slow or "lazy" might really mean that you are lucky as hell. Lucky to trust in the pacing that feels right to you without regard for what society would decide is best for you. The world wants to sell you quick fixes, but that's not what the Pacing Pursuit phase is all about. It's about pacing yourself toward the warmth of sun.

Two other options related to pacing are available as well:

- *Pause*
- *Choose to change course*

Sometimes you just need to pause and catch your breath. Since my soul awakening, I've chosen to take two very different kinds of pauses. First, when I could not figure out if retiring from my corporate life was even the right decision, I requested and was granted an eight-week sabbatical. I had never asked for a pause like that. But being able to pause and give myself the time and space I needed to find clarity was exactly what I needed to keep me growing forward. By the end of my time out, both my employer and I had more clarity, and the decision was made that I would retire. Was that a simple decision? *Absolutely not.* But were we able to get there by giving ourselves a pause for a time out? *Yes.*

Second, during the writing of this very book, I was knee-deep in planning *Ready or Not* (known as RON 2.0), a women's event I created and now co-produce with my podcast co-host, Wendy.

RON 2.0 is an afternoon packed with locally sourced speakers. It's a time when women of our community come together and focus on three things—growth, connection, and joy! It's a labor of love to put it together, but when the room is full of women who get the Seeker mindset, it's 100% worth it.

I was feeling torn between writing and hosting, and even though I knew my heart was in both places, I knew that for this book to grow into what I knew it could, I needed to request a pause. And sure enough, even when my editor had concerns about losing my writing momentum, I listened to my voice that said *take a break*. I took two months off from focusing any of my time and attention to my second book "baby." When the time was up, I returned ready to keep writing. And I finished the book you have in your hands right this very moment!

I include those examples so you know that if you truly want what you say you want, it's okay to change your pacing over time. Let time take time. Listen to your voice. And trust that even though it might not be easy to get back to work, you have the tools to ease back in by choosing actions that feel safe and simple, moving forward one step (or one word) at a time.

Before I dive more deeply into the option of changing course (which we will learn more about in the Rooting Trust phase of the Growth Cycle in the next chapter), let me share one last piece of my running story to get us over the finish line on pacing. I haven't run a mile or even a fraction of that in months, maybe even a year. Just because I had a dream for growth once doesn't mean that I have to stay with it for the rest of my life, ramping up and up and up. I don't have to link my identity to my intermittent hopes. I can simply use them as an opportunity for growth at that time. I can take those learnings on through my next adventure, however.

Changing course and allowing some roots to run deeper while others end shallower doesn't make you a quitter. It doesn't make you lazy. It means that you are a learner, a grower, and a master YOU-Turner. It means that you can *choose* to change course completely.

But we'll save that for the next chapter.

The tool you need to add to your toolkit now is to shift from all-or-nothing thinking (meaning you are either growing or not growing) to a confident, self-aware, self-paced, grace-packed, bundle of growth, connection, and joy-seeking kind of human.

That's who I know you can be. Shoot, that might be exactly who you are right now.

Tool for Practice

PAUSE TO PACE

Pacing yourself is about consistently monitoring how you are growing IRL. Give yourself permission to take a quick pause to check in with yourself and either keep mental notes or journal so that you can look for opportunities to push harder or pull back and care for yourself as best you can. This Tool for Practice is yet another opportunity for you to give yourself the time you deserve for self-reflection, then allow what you learn to help you choose your next inspired action.

Take three deep breaths, then ask yourself the following questions. I invite you to close your eyes, ask each question, and see what answer presents itself as you engage in a one-woman (or man) conversation on pacing.

* Do I feel appropriately paced (a.k.a., Am I growing too slow, too fast, or not at all)?

* Do I feel the need to pull back, slow down, push harder and try more, or hold steady?

* Do I need to take a pause or break?

* If so, when will I commit to checking back in with myself to see if I'm ready to return?

* How can I best honor what my soul is telling me?

Whatever answers come back to you, do your best to trust them rather than judge them. If you feel tired but your heart says it's still time to push, trust that. Then make a plan to rest and recover as soon as the push is over. If you feel physically and mentally strong but you have no spark of inspiration for your current goal, let it rest awhile. Revisit it after a defined period of time that feels right. Report back to yourself.

Trust your gut when it says it's go-time and when it says you're a no-go. It will take practice to know when you might need to speed up, slow down, pause, or change course. And even though your goals seem like they can hardly wait for you to conquer them, trust me that slow and steady consistency will help you grow in the right direction—the direction of your choosing toward your Inspired Life!

I look back on my own growth and see how I've built up my endurance and stamina for challenges of all kinds (emotional, intellectual, physical) over the years, and I'm proud of that improvement, but hear me again when I say it has taken time and multiple trial-and-error periods with different paces.

I'm proud of the times I have pushed myself hard, and I'm proud of the times I napped like a boss. I'm proud of the fact that I can watch and admire other Seekers growing at their own pace and not get sucked into comparison or jealousy. Learning how to safely grow throughout the Pacing Pursuit phase is one that will serve you well. You've got a long, Inspired Life ahead of you, so learning how to keep things safe and simple while pacing yourself is key to sustained growth.

And now that you've grown through the first three phases of the Growth Cycle, it's time to enter the last phase—Rooting Trust—where you'll learn about what it takes to foster a solid foundation to hold your soul steady!

SHIFTING SOIL

ROOTING TRUST

THE *Growth* CYCLE

BREAKING THROUGH

PACING PURSUIT

Chapter 8

GROWTH CYCLE PHASE 4

ROOTING TRUST

Do you trust yourself?

It might seem like an odd question, but it's one that if you can't confidently answer *Yes!*, then we know there is still work to do. But here's the thing: If you have to stop and think about this question, you are normal. All too many times, we make decisions for ourselves, but we double back and question our judgment. The goal, though, is that as you show up as the Seeker you choose to be, over time you will find more confidence in yourself. You *will* trust yourself.

In *The Thin Book of Trust*, Charles Feltman defines trust in a way that changed my world. His book was written in the context of building trust in the workplace, but his way of looking at trust changed my view of my own trust relationship with myself. He asserts that trust is *choosing* to risk something you value and making it vulnerable to another person's actions. Conversely, he defines distrust as what is valuable to me is not safe with this person in this situation (or any situation). When I read his thin book (trust me and him, it's more like a pamphlet… and I highly recommend reading it), I realized that one of the most important choices I will make time and time again is this: Will I choose to trust myself and risk the safety and security I might be currently enjoying to explore my options and venture out of my comfort zone toward growth?

When I truly look back at my growth journey, much of the heartache, the willingness to stay stuck, settling for less than I knew my soul wanted, was because I simply didn't trust myself to grow. I didn't trust that I could keep myself safe through life-altering change. I valued my sense of security so much that I simply couldn't (and wouldn't) choose to make that security vulnerable to the new choices I knew I'd have to make to keep growing.

For many years, I distrusted my own gut because I just didn't know if I could keep myself safe.

But that's what the Rooting Trust phase is all about. It's time to take what we've learned and complete the Growth Cycle, to focus on how we can root our growth journey in trust. It's time to learn how to ground ourselves in our own internal wisdom through discernment-generating exploration. It's time to start spreading your roots and in doing so, rooting yourself in a whole new level of self-trust.

What Is Rooting Trust

This phase of the Growth Cycle is all about allowing yourself to continue to embrace the exploration required to grow while building a solid foundation of self-trust that will fuel your sustained Seeker-hood. Rooting Trust means embracing your unique and ever-evolving journey as well as expanding your comfort zone. It's about growing more and more grounded in certain truths of your ability to live, learn, and find your truth.

As you find the rhythm of growth that works for you and as you trust your own path, the opportunities to try new things will always show up. You just have to decide whether you're ready and willing to try any of them. Everything is a learning opportunity—some more exciting than others, some more challenging than others. So, the choice you have is to ride the highs, push through the lows, be willing to try, and grow, grow, grow.

Easing your way out of an all-or-nothing mentality or fixed mindset that has fueled you for years will not be the simplest of tasks. It's going to take time, energy, and effort to grow into a more confident try-er.

If you choose to try, odds are you won't die (unless you try big-risk undertakings, like skydiving, but I think even that is mostly safe). Odds are you will survive whatever experience you are contemplating. Odds are you will come out the other side. So again, why not try?

If you choose to be willing to make your sense of safety, security, and certainty vulnerable to a new experience time and time again, day in and day out, I guarantee that the odds are absolutely in your favor that you will rise to new accomplishments, begin to trust yourself more, and your Inspired Life will keep taking shape.

This phase is about giving yourself permission to spread grounding roots of trust, knowing that some roots might grow deeper and deeper, while others might stay shallow or stop growing because they have reached their natural end. If you were to look at the root structure of a tree you'd see a mingling of roots of all sizes, shapes, and depths. We are no different. We have to spread roots that can firmly hold us in the ground, but we also need smaller roots that create a beautiful tapestry of the Growth Cycle in action. Some of our roots are pretty straight and strong, others are weaker and curly. But each root has its own story to tell, its own lesson learned, and its own importance in your personal journey.

Rooting Trust can and should be *fun*, powered by your curiosity, and the spirit that you can't know unless you try.

Rooting Trust is about building a solid network below you so that it can nurture any longed-for growth up and out into this world. During this phase you'll have the opportunity to chart your own course, plant your own seeds, and watch how they grow. Along the way, you'll learn how to make adjustments so that you can keep growing forward in healthy, life-giving ways. You'll learn how to continue to challenge yourself and your self-imposed limitations.

Allowing roots of trust to spread and take hold will require patience just like the other phases. We will have to keep letting time take time. But especially in this phase, growth is all about embracing the time it takes to explore, about rooting around and pushing through new soil, and about giving yourself time to see how your energy, passion, and vigor can help move you forward. At the same time, we will also keep in mind that not all growth is healthy, strong, and life-giving. Not all growth is meant to last. So, it's in this final phase of the Growth Cycle where you'll have the chance to grow wiser through trial and error and gain some serious discernment skills. It might sound daunting, but in the end, it's empowering. For now, remember this:

You are safe.

You have options.

And you can trust that you are safe with your choices.

It is those truths that we'll spend time with now to make sure they are planted firmly in your heart because they are the root of this phase of the Growth Cycle. Your truths will tell you how to keep growing toward your Inspired Life!

What Rooting Trust Looks and Feels Like

When I left my first career in 2018, I had wistful dreams of launching my company, Dena Speaks. I imagined I'd become a professional speaker, working with women who were longing to be empowered or with businesses that were into the "soft skills" that my profession at the time didn't focus on. My dream was personal and professional development in the areas of trust, values-based business, and people—really, anything that had to do with helping people show up for themselves and their potential in more intentional ways.

When asked what I was going to do, the big idea in my mind was that I'd somehow go out and inspire the masses (yes, I know that sounds corny, but it was my truth). I had a few grand visions of myself walking onto giant stages across the U.S. at company conferences or large gatherings of women as the attendees sat in their seats and the hot, white lights followed me as I shared powerful words of wisdom about how I believed that each and every one of them could create the life of their dreams. I wanted to inspire them, to make them curious, and to leave them with some nugget of wisdom, some spark of hope that would lead them to make some change, any change for the better for themselves.

I wanted to help people help themselves. That dream was so deeply rooted in my heart that it gave me the courage to leave corporate life and the security it provided to my family.

But once I ventured into the world of entrepreneurship, I started to realize that it wasn't just the dream of creating a business that was truly my life-force. My true life-force was the power to create my Inspired Life based on my ability to make new choices for myself. That's why after only a couple of months after walking out of corporate life, I trusted my gut that I in fact did *not* want to expand as a speaking business that would lead me to board planes, trains, and Ubers. I realized that all of it would take me away from my family, something I knew wasn't right for me (or them) at that time.

I was sure I wanted to be at home every morning to see my kiddos and make their lunches before they went off to school. I also knew I wanted to retreat to the recesses of my brain and write a book. And not only a book, but a memoir where I'd look back at my life and truly reflect on all I'd lived and learned. I didn't know how exactly to make my publishing dreams come true, but I trusted that I could figure it out. That's what my heart wanted. It's where my energy longed to be directed.

Was I letting the dream of building a business die? *No.*

Was I exploring what was possible for me? *Yes.*

Was it comfortable for me? *Nope, not always.*

But did I trust it was the right move? *Yes.*

For me and my Inspired Life, first came the huge transition away from my prior corporate work, then a slow unraveling of what my body and brain knew about how to exist. I had such well-worn patterns of corporate life that my leap out of one career and into a very different next phase of life turned into an amazing opportunity to slow down. JP and I would joke that it was taking me years to unwind myself from all the years of go-go-go. And in slowing down, I was able to explore at my own pace what felt right to me, and just as important, what didn't feel right to me.

And to this day, I continue to embrace the living and learning of every new choice I make. I am putting down roots all around my soul as I embrace choosing to trust myself. Some roots are running deep and holding me steady—like the roots in my choice to wake up every day and be the best Seeker I can be, the roots to see everything I do as an opportunity to learn something, and the roots in the belief that I matter and my life has meaning and purpose. Other roots, like building a booming business, have stayed shallow, veering off the side as they try to find footing or might eventually stop.

I remind myself that no root is too short or too long. No root is worthless. Every growth has been worth what is happening—I'm finding the people, places, and things that help me feel grounded in my self-created reality and have tapped into the natural nutrients that I need to feel alive and inspired. What it all reminds me of is this: Just like every precious seed grows up and out into the world, all the while it grows roots down below. So do our souls.

As I consider my roots—those I want, those I'm working on, roots in self-confidence, self-compassion, and self-trust—I imagine my soul with this beautiful tangle of roots down below that have all different sizes, shapes, and depths. I focus on how they all funnel back to fuel me with more knowledge and wisdom to answer what you already know I believe is one of life's most important questions—*What do I want?*

How to Get Firmly Rooted in Trust

Think back to the beginning of this book and your Seeker Statement. When you gave yourself time to dream up those desires, it might have felt daunting to think about how you'd make progress toward what you wanted. But after acknowledging the Shifting Soil, you decided in the Breaking Through phase to take action, and you have been Pacing Pursuit. And all the while, you have been spreading roots in new behaviors that will serve you as the Seeker you are choosing to be. You might have already started to ask yourself questions like *is this the right way to grow?* If you have, your longing to grow is real, and it's totally normal to want to get it right. But when you start to ponder that question, let me share three truths that will serve you and help you root your personal growth journey in self-trust:

1. There is no one way to get there (wherever "there" is).

I know it's hard not to compare yourself to others, thinking that there is one "right" way to do things, but trust me, there is no one, single, or same way that everyone achieves personal success, fulfillment, and sustained health and joy. Seekers are not doing all the exact same things. Every person is different and so are their growth journeys. The diversity is a huge part of what makes the world a beautiful place to live in.

When we're knee-deep in a transition of our own, it gets scary and it can make a lot of sense to try to simply follow in someone else's footsteps, trusting the paths they have plotted before us. We think because if it worked for them, surely it will work for us. I say go ahead and follow a few steps along their path. If it's a similar venture, their path very well might work.

Really, though, this phase of the Growth Cycle gives *you* the opportunity to explore and learn what works for you. And in that exploration, you'll have chance after chance to build the trust you have in your own instincts. That trust will take time and experience to build. The roots you are spreading will have twists and turns and even some dead ends. But all of those outcomes are essential opportunities for living and learning.

If you keep showing up with humble curiosity and everyday bravery, you can and will figure out your way and find the fun in trusting your *own* way.

2. *No one knows the way except for you.*

While it would be nice to chase your dreams while walking, jogging, or running on a well-worn path that others have created, that route isn't likely the one that will lead to *your* Inspired Life. My best advice to you is to forge your own path and see every step you take as an opportunity to choose your next move for yourself. There is no one who can know your way except you.

As you share your Seeker Statement or even just begin to open your mind to change, there will be people who think and believe that they know just what you should do next. People you love and care for will hear what you are dreaming up and have thoughts, feelings, concerns, and well-thought-out (or not so well-thought-out) opinions about your ability to make your ideas become a reality, along with ideas to get there from where you are today, who you should go to for support and guidance, and the list will go on and on.

Kudos to you, though, for trusting yourself to be brave and vulnerable if you chose to share your hopes for change with another or others. But that second truth above is all about what happens after that phase. Indeed, it's most beneficial for your growth to simply hear what they have to say, taking it for what it's worth, as information to consider and explore, not required action or gospel truth. Odds are the person(s) you shared with wishes you well. Most likely, they want you to succeed. But despite all their best intentions, take all the guidance, advice, or musings you receive with a grain of gracious salt. Why?

No one knows the way except for you.

You will have to judge for yourself what you hold on to or what you let go. As you progress through the Growth Cycle, you'll learn to discern with greater levels of confidence in your ability to judge well and choose your next inspired steps forward.

3. *The route (and the exact destination) can and will change over time.*

To say that life is full of surprises is a huge understatement. Chasing goals, dreams, and changes for the better is no different. Growth can be messy above ground where you can see plants get unruly as well as below ground where you can't see the roots growing out, around, and over each other as each vies for position. You can count on zigs and zags along your way, too. On one or many days, you'll feel like everything is going smoothly, then *wham!* something pops up and throws it all out of whack. Anticipate as best as possible that the route you choose for your growth can and will change over time. And the sooner you embrace that truth, the less frustrating your efforts will be.

Another piece of this truth that becomes clearer is that even while you might change your chosen routes, the actual dreams for your Inspired Life themselves can change. The changes we long for evolve as we do. They grow up along with us. Or sometimes we even grow out of them. Adaptation is normal and natural. Let me share an example from my own life to help drive home this point.

In 2018, I worked for months creating *Ready or Not*, RON as it was lovingly abbreviated to, as a first-of-its kind women's conference for my local community. I dreamed up an afternoon of talks and workshops all about growth, connection, and joy. After months of planning, networking, double-checking, and dreaming, it was ready to go. Then in January 2019, as I stood on the RON stage that first year, I can describe it as nothing other than an out-of-body experience. I was aware of everything, proud of everything, floating through the real-life experience that I'd been dreaming of for months.

Year two in 2020 brought about another first as the event sold out and adding five more women speakers to the lineup. They spoke about their struggles and how they chose to show up and grow in their own unique ways. They laughed, cried, and created a safe place where the women who came could relax, let down their guards, and soak up wisdom from the women of their very own community.

I heard nothing but great things from sponsors and attendees. It was clearly a success. But oddly I felt a nagging sense of disappointment. I sat with the feelings for months before doing a solid 12 pages of journaling, trying to figure out what I learned, what I hoped for the future, and what I'd do differently going forward. In a nutshell, all my self-reflection highlighted that I simply wanted more time on stage, sharing my heart with the goal of impacting women. But even more than that, I was longing for a partner or team to share it with. I was disappointed that I didn't have anyone to share my passion for creating the event and witnessing its impact. In hindsight, it was a first whisper of shifting soil in my soul.

Then COVID hit and threw us all a curveball we hadn't seen coming. I made the decision to take RON virtual in 2021. I ramped up the amazing speaker lineup to over 10 badass women who brought recorded words of wisdom to nearly 100 women who joined in from actual coast to coast. I learned a ton. I invested time, money, and energy into it. Women were engaged, and the stories we heard of impact made it all worth it. But my experience of it still fell flat. This work on something that I loved and believed in so much was not resonating with my truth.

When it came time to make a decision on whether I'd create and promote a fourth year of *Ready or Not*, I kept procrastinating. While I was on a call with my life coach one afternoon, she finally asked me what I was going to do about the conference. I told her that I was going to put RON on hold and not produce it. As soon as the words left my mouth, so did what felt like a million pounds of pressure.

"What do you want to do then?" she asked me.

"I want to write," I said. Tears welled up in my eyes as my truth was set free. It's amazing what honest expression can do for the soul. These tears were not for sadness—they were for authenticity. Happy tears. Real tears.

At that moment I knew that it was time for one dream to take a back seat and another to take over in the driver's seat. This book was ready to be written. It was time for me to trust in three things I'm sharing with you now.

- I had to trust that there was no one way to grow forward.
- I had to trust that no one knew the way except for me.
- And I had to trust that the route toward my Inspired Life can and would change and that the dreams themselves could and would also evolve over time.

And the crazy thing is that after taking an entire year off from RON and after having completed the first draft of this book, I was ready to bring RON back… but only if I had a partner. So, in 2023, a slightly rebranded, but majorly reinvigorated, RON 2.0 hit the stage, when Wendy, my podcast co-host, who also became my event co-producer, and I welcomed 200 women (the largest crowd to date) from our community. The energy was electric, and the growth was epic. The root that had been my first several years of RON might have ended, but then RON 2.0 began its own growth journey.

The thing that really grew—and what really matters in the Rooting Trust phase—is the level of trust I had in my own heart and soul. Heightened trust is what Seekers want in this final phase of the Growth Cycle—to keep grounding ourselves in the truth that we can trust ourselves as we grow. It's all about becoming more confident, more capable, and more rooted in your ability to create your Inspired Life. Self-trust builds over time, and it builds through experience.

Be Willing to Try

If the three truths I just shared hold—which I assert firmly that they do—then there is one choice that will root you in fertile trust-enriched soil for growth. It's a choice you will have to make over and over again: *You must choose to show up and be willing to try.*

This mantra should be said out loud: *I can't know if I don't try.*

I almost want to stop this chapter right now. Because those words contain the real kicker when it comes to this phase of the Growth Cycle. Remember the humble curiosity that Seekers show up with? The humble part is just as important as the curiosity.

You can't know everything there is to know.

Similarly, there are things that you simply just don't know *yet*. And maybe you don't know them because you haven't had the opportunity to learn them, or you have been blind to the learning in front of you. Maybe it's that you have been assuming you know something from watching rather than doing, or you have been fearful and refused to put yourself out there to live and learn. Don't beat yourself up. While you can't know everything, here's what you can know. You are capable of navigating change. You are capable of trying new things. And you are capable of applying whatever nuggets of knowledge you glean while trying to do those new things.

You can (and will) learn—if you are willing to try.

Try saying this simple statement: *It is fun to learn.*

Did you choke on those words, or did they roll right off your tongue with ease?

As your elementary school teachers likely told you: Learning can be fun! Some people seem to inherently understand that concept (and better than others). Those who get it naturally are typically the ones who jump right into new experiences. They make it seem so easy. They just don't struggle to find the will to try new things. I tend to be the exception. For me at least, learning new things is not something I naturally gravitate toward as a "fun" thing to do. I get nervous and anxious, and I tell myself that I cannot learn the new thing, that the new thing is really hard. That pattern of thought used to hold me back and kept me feeling stuck.

But once I chose to be a Seeker and nurture my own soul toward the Inspired Life I longed for, I got better and better at growing scared. Then over time, I learned how to slow down my fear-based, fixed-mindset brain. I learned it's okay to not always know what is going to happen. I learned to take a breath and do my darnedest to accept that learning can be fun. I also learned to frame experiences as opportunities to gain a new skill set, push past the negative and self-imposed, self-limiting beliefs, and just try the darn thing.

This area of growth will continue to be an exercise of gathering your courage, humility, and sense of humor by repeating over and over and over again:

It's fun to learn.
It's fun to learn.
It's fun to learn.

Think of it this way: Not only is it actually fun to learn, but you *get to* learn. That small shift in mindset from you *have to* learn to you *get to* learn might be all you need to stay the course. How freaking fortunate are you that you are still alive, kicking, and *get to* try all the things as you keep growing?

Stay alert, however, for mental, fear-inducing stop signs. You know…the ones that suggest you're not ready, the ones that flash WAIT! When you see those in your mind's eye, stay curious and ask yourself *are you holding yourself back from something you want because you aren't 100% ready?* I get it. For many, many years of my life I didn't take chances, didn't put myself out there, and didn't dare risk my reputation or ego all because of the chance that I might fail.

That inertia changed for me once I realized that no one has it all figured out and that no one is ever 100% ready (hence the name *Ready or Not*). Not one person knows all there is to know about everything. Moreover, there is no one out there living life perfectly. We're all flying by the seats of our pants. But if we will just try, then we *can* learn. We—you, me, everyone really—will always learn *something in the process.*

Back to the essence of creating your Inspired Life: You can't know if you don't try.

Take hope-fueled action. Take safe, simple risks. Place small, yet meaningful bets on yourself and your courage as well as on your capability to survive the unknown. You can learn and grow. And when something doesn't go well (or it's painful and downright sucks), do this:

Let it suck. Then learn from it.

Revisit the Get a G.R.I.P. steps from Chapter 6. *Give your emotions time and space.* Feel the not-so-fun emotions when things don't go your way, cry the tears, throw things (in a safe way, of course), curl up in the ball, and eat the ice cream. Then *regulate your breathing, imagine other options,* and *pause and circle back* as you find something to learn from the experience.

Think about what went right, what went wrong, what you could change next time, and what you can still be proud of…

reflect and learn. Then whether it's a seemingly big or small loss, whether it was rejection, doubt, or fear that knocked you down, pick yourself up, dry your tears, and keep looking up and out, not down and around. Trust your path, pace yourself, and be willing to keep trying.

Each new day is a new chance to make choices that will serve you better. The question you'll have to ask yourself is *will you try again?* Can you handle the slips and surges sure to come your way if you keep showing up as a Seeker? If you can't succeed or win, will you abandon the attempt? If something doesn't come naturally, will you bail or try again?

Hint: Don't give up. Practice the following Tool for Practice to build self-trust with each successful or unsuccessful attempt and trust that you can keep growing.

Tool for Practice

TRYING FOR TRUST

Let's revisit the question that kicked off this chapter: *Do you trust yourself?* I truly believe that your answer will become more affirmative the more time and energy you give to trying new things, things your heart and soul are guiding you toward.

So, for a few moments, I want you to think about trying for trust. And here's a new way to guide your efforts on this topic: the 3 Rs—rest, reflect, and reaffirm. Those three powerful steps will help you as you keep choosing to try something new and trust yourself more and more.

This exercise can take five minutes or five hours… you decide how long you need. The only rule is to limit self-judgment; simply notice what comes up for you.

Step 1: Rest

Slow down. Take a few deep breaths and recover from what is probably the increased speed of your life from the growth you've already experienced. Find a way to join yourself in the "here and now" in a calm, safe place!

Step 2: Reflect

Reflect on these questions/prompts:

* Think back on your Seeker Statement, Dream Day Exercise, Personal Manifesto, or your overall vision for your Inspired Life. Has anything about them changed?

* Jot down what things you have tried so far to move closer to what you want. What things worked, what didn't? What did you learn?

* Recall any particular highs or lows you experienced as you tried new things and what you have learned from both.

* Were there times you questioned yourself? If so, jot down why you were unsure.

* Did you find it hard to choose to make yourself vulnerable to your own actions?

* If you are finding it easier to trust yourself and make your sense of security vulnerable to trying new things, to what can you attribute that growing trust relationship?

Step 3: Reaffirm

Life, as well as living happily, is about choices. Take what you've learned from Step 2 and make sure you are still headed down the path that feels right to you. Close your eyes and ask yourself, "Am I growing in the right direction? Can I make a conscious choice to trust myself?"

You can use the 3 Rs tool as often as it feels necessary to keep connecting with yourself throughout the Rooting Trust phase, or really any phase of the Growth Cycle. There's never a wrong time to rest, reflect, and reaffirm, to see what clarity you can find. Then commit to trusting yourself to keep trying and make changes you decide are necessary to keep growing in the right direction toward your Inspired Life!

Having lived and learned through the entire Growth Cycle and both the *Plant* and *Grow* sections of this book, it's time to move onto the final section and well-known farming season that always comes with much hope and anticipation—*Harvest*!

Harvest

Chapter 9
BEGIN AND END WITH CELEBRATION

A t the end of growing season every year on the farm, there is the much-anticipated harvest. After months of hard work and dedication, it's finally time to gather whatever crop might have been produced and bring that cycle to a close. I've spent the last two decades watching my husband gear up and plant a crop, then nurture and help it grow from seed to harvest. Over the years, I have seen that harvest time can often feel like the most delicate time because there seems to be so much riding on the results of the harvest.

For JP, it's a business (like most businesses) with so many variables at play: crop markets (how much the crop is worth this year), crop production (how bountiful the plants ended up being), and layered on top of both is the need to have weather and conditions cooperate in order to even get the crop out of the field.

I've watched him work in fields full of cotton that were considered bumper crops with commodity prices high enough to potentially yield meaningful profit, but then have hurricane season swing in and throw off severe storms with damaging winds and hail that come through, nearly breaking my farmer's heart. In these moments, he's fretted, fussed, and waded in frustration.

I've watched him put out literal fires in their cotton stripper. (Side note: It is always fun to talk about the "stripper," as we call it, around people who have no clue that it's just what they call that beast of a harvesting machine.), then get back in the next day and keep those wheels rolling, trusting that it was "go-time."

But I've also watched him pop bottles of champagne and spray his farm partner and father as they celebrate a bumper crop that was harvested without any major hitches. He put in the hours, the heart, and that year was blessed with a harvest he remembers to this day.

And I've seen some years that don't have any intense highs or lows, but rather just a consistent push to gather all the crops that he can, do his best to wrap up one season, only to take a short pause and get ready for the next.

Really, there's only one constant: harvest happens. It just doesn't always look the same, feel the same, or yield the same results. But at the end of every period of growth there is an opportunity to gather the goods, take stock of what's been learned, review what was tried, celebrate what worked, and take note of what didn't.

That's what this final section of the book will give you—tools you can use to harvest your own amazing growth! And there's no better place to start than to trust that you must begin and end with celebration!

Celebrate Your Growth Journey

When was the last time you felt really proud of yourself?

With fingers and toes crossed, I hope that it doesn't take long for you to conjure up a smile and a memory of the last time you stopped and were like, *"Yeah, I just did that! I am amazing!"*

But in my experience, many newly awakened (and even veteran) Seekers haven't quite gotten the healthy pattern of self-praise down. Odds are any moments of pride that surface are focused on your kids, teammates, work colleagues, or someone that is not you (and you alone). And that's okay. How wonderful that we can be proud of the accomplishments of others.

But this book isn't about them, it's about YOU! You've chosen to be a Seeker. You've dreamed up your Inspired Life. You've prioritized yourself through YOU-Turns as you managed growing pains. You have lots to be proud of! And the truth is that you do have something to be proud of. You just haven't practiced celebrating yourself enough.

And even if you have been able to give yourself some celebratory attention, there is a good chance that you tend to focus on all that you haven't yet accomplished. Our tendency is to wait to celebrate until we hit the goal or reach the finish line. But that's a habit that won't serve us in the long run. Because here's the thing (and I share this with the scary teeth-exposed emoji face taking over my real face): There is no singular moment of arrival. So, if you keep postponing celebrating yourself, you'll be depriving yourself of the recognition and praise that all your hard work deserves!

As a Seeker, you are committed to the pursuit of your potential to become an even better version of yourself than you are right now. Even when you have very specific goals that you are chasing or very real dreams you long for in your Inspired Life, if—wait, scratch *if—when* you reach them, life still goes on, you still have more life in you, and your heart is still beating.

That's why learning how to embrace the ever-repeating

Harvest phase is imperative. You don't just reach a pinnacle and stop growing. You simply have a higher, more evolved, more ful-filled, and wiser point of view and perspective from which you now live life. And then you get to choose again whether you will keep growing.

In your choice to keep growing, you also have to know that every harvest will be different. And over time, your dreams, goals, hopes, and longings will change because you change. But if we never stop to celebrate how far we've come, then we are missing the point entirely.

Growth should be fun!

Physically, mentally, and emotionally taxing? *Yes.* Comfort-zone expanding? *Mm-hmm.* Identity-shifting? *Yup.* Confidence-boosting? *You better believe it!*

So, is growth worth it? *Absolutely.* And anything worth doing is 100% worth celebrating.

Sometimes, though, we diminish the importance of celebrat-ing. When I work with coaching clients, part of our standard rhythm is to begin and end each meeting with celebrations. It goes like this.

"Tell me what you are proud of or want to be celebrated for?"

Awkward silences normally fill the seconds after that. Or there's some hemming and hawing as they rack their brain for something. I might even get my most dreaded response, "I can't think of anything," which means we have some serious celebration training to do.

I poke around a bit and ask some questions until we find something, anything that they can celebrate for themselves, even if it's just the fact that they were on the call and didn't bail out.

There is nothing too small to celebrate. And here are several fun examples:

- *I reached out to an old friend who I'd been thinking about a lot lately.*
- *I soaked extra-long in my bathtub last night after a crappy day.*
- *I bought/listened to/read a new book for fun or to learn something new.*
- *I turned in the assignment that I'd been procrastinating about finishing.*
- *I talked to my husband/partner/spouse about something that was bothering me.*
- *I did some research on job openings that intrigue me.*
- *I went to a movie by myself.*
- *I hired a new virtual assistant and trained her on what I want her to do.*
- *I went and saw my therapist.*
- *I tried a new restaurant in town.*

All those things are worth celebrating! Why? Because they were important to the women who did them, and they honored their own experiences. They are proud of themselves for doing something either they needed to do, wanted to do, never had done, finally got the courage up to do, or simply felt ready to do.

Then 60 or 90 minutes later as we wrap up our time together before they dive back into their real life, I ask again, "Okay, so tell me now, even just this short bit of time later, what do you want to celebrate?"

And do you want to know the most common answer I hear back? Okay, I'll tell you:

"I'm proud of myself for showing up today. For giving myself this time to focus on myself."

That single celebration never surprises me; it only makes me smile and reminds me that so many women have work to do when it comes to prioritizing their growth! And over time, my clients become better and better cheerleaders for themselves and their growth. It makes me so proud when I see someone not only learning how to be proud of themselves but embracing that self-pride and using it as fuel to keep growing.

I'll say it again because I think it's vital in the Harvest phase—there is nothing too small to celebrate. After committing to a change for the better for yourself and showing up consistently, there comes a time when you finally embrace the importance of celebrating the process, not just any resulting outcome. Making the life of your dreams become a reality is about progress, not just the final destination.

That's why every single day, you can focus on finding something to celebrate. It might be that you responded differently to a situation than you normally would, that you said yes to something you never would have before, that you took a nap, or that you cried to a friend. Every single time you arrive at a new healthier-for-you pattern of behavior or a new-to-you learning moment, you have something to cheer about.

You are changing like a champ. You are growing like a freaking beast! All those everyday brave baby steps are turning into leaps of faith as you hurdle toward a deeper sense of self-knowing. I'm proud of you just thinking about it. I want you to be proud too.

Let celebration be something you practice frequently because growth isn't easy. You might have an end in your mind's eye as you focus on your Inspired Life, but if you don't stop to celebrate growth along the way, you might find fatigue setting in. Celebration is a way to refuel your little tank with hope and optimism and pride.

I have a picture that my husband took of me years ago. It was the second day of my sabbatical. I'd surprised my hubby with a quick getaway to a cool hotel not far from us. The sun had set, and as I sat fully clothed on a pool lounger, I kicked off my shoes, laid back, and closed my eyes, listening to the waterfall. For some reason, it felt right to extend my hands backward and give a double dose of the middle finger. My husband snapped the picture, and it's perfect.

It captured for me a milestone moment in my life. I look at the Dena in that picture, and I am so proud of her. At that point in her professional transition, she still didn't know what she was going to do—would she stay or would she go? She still didn't know exactly what she wanted to create in a business. She still didn't know what all that change would mean for her family. There were so many things she didn't know.

But she did know this: She had listened to her voice saying that she needed to take a break so she could find clarity. She had been brave enough to say *what if I took a sabbatical? What if I completely changed my pace for just a bit? What if I take some time so that we can try to find the answers that are eluding us?* And as she sat chilling her wound-way-too-tight butt in that chair, she'd arrived. She'd asked for what she needed and felt a moment of calm and peace. She trusted that everything would work out in the end even though she still didn't have all the answers. She knew she'd grown, and she wanted to give the real world a big old middle finger, telling it to eff off and hang tight while she paced herself.

I was proud of myself. If I'd waited an additional two years to retire from my corporate gig, I don't know that I would have made the change. Okay, so maybe I would have, but I sure as heck wouldn't have learned how important it was to begin and end with a celebration and even fill up all the middle parts with applause as well. Because, dang it, I was growing, which deserved a hip-hip-hooray. And you are growing too, and you deserve a cheer as well!

My confident guess is that you have changed from the person you were when you starting reading this book. You've figured something out about yourself. You've grown just a smidge more confident about who you are, what you want, and why that matters. I'm proud of you. Now, the work is for you to focus on being proud of yourself. There is nothing too small to celebrate. So begin and end each day, each transition, each big decision, or each change with 'atta-girls galore.

While you're at it, find a little fun by exploring different ways to praise yourself. If you want to go the no-money-down version, just sit silently and have quiet moments of self-reflection on your growth. Make your way to a local farmer's market and just walk the aisles appreciating what other people are growing! You could go to a public park and try out a new hike or take a blanket and have a precious little picnic. You might even celebrate by getting rid of something old. It might sound odd, but what if you celebrated learning something new by filling up a bag with items to donate? Clear your home, car, or workspace and free up some mental and physical space for the new perspectives on your horizon. You could also just text or tell a friend the next time you experience yourself change for the better. Whatever you try, remember that celebration doesn't have to cost anything. It's priceless!

If you feel like treating yourself to something, remember that it doesn't have to be "big"—maybe a new water bottle, new Sharpies, or a killer multicolor pack of sticky notes might just do the trick. Then use them to write yourself a note of congratulations that might simply say *I Did That!* Buy a frame to display a picture of a special milestone you reached that filled you with pride. Got your eye on a new yoga mat or new tech gadget? Go for it if it will bring you joy and remind you of what it is you are celebrating—yourself and your commitment to growth!

Trust your path and celebrate often. You are doing work that no one else can do for you, so honor your commitment and find the power in well-earned self-pride and praise. Just remember it's all about controlling what you can control—your commitment to seeing what you can live and learn for yourself, what adjustments you can make to keep growing toward your Inspired Life, prioritizing yourself with YOU-Turns, and nurturing yourself through the Growth Cycle. Harvest is all about gathering and celebrating the fruits of your labor, so be sure to try this Tool for Practice to help you take your celebration skills to the next level.

Tool for Practice

CHEER YOURSELF ON

You must learn to celebrate yourself—over and over again. As you grow choice by choice, experience by experience, you have the chance to bolster yourself up by celebrating all you've learned. And there is no better feeling than a true, deep sense of self-pride. One of the best characteristics that we can model for those we love, care for, and work with is a humble, yet pride-filled sense of self-love. Because in those moments, we give others permission to do the same.

In this Tool for Practice, it's time to Cheer Yourself On as you keep growing. Notice that I did not say that I encourage you to go find ways to be a cocky, arrogant butthead. Nope, that's not what I said. I also did not say to celebrate the *thing* you might have achieved or the *thing* you bought or obtained. That's not what I meant. Cheering yourself on is all about you—the person—finding a humble and gracious spirit within yourself and acknowledging all the everyday brave steps you've taken to grow.

The first few times that you celebrate a particular act might feel strange, so I simply invite you to become more aware of opportunities to celebrate yourself. And there's no better time than right now to stop and finish this sentence:

I am proud of myself for ...

If you happen to find yourself stumped or want to dig in a bit more, here are a few specific questions you can ask yourself. The answers to them are all facets you should be proud of and celebrate!

* What change have I seen in myself that makes me proud and excited?

* How do I experience life differently now than I have before?

* What are things I struggled with before but now maybe less or not at all?

* What are some of the most fun things I've lived and learned recently?

* What am I most excited to try and conquer or grow toward next?

Maybe you went in a different direction on your walk this morning to prove to yourself that you can in fact change your routines. Maybe you made a call that just thinking about made your stomach do flip-flops, but you dialed the number and let it ring. Maybe you said no to a prospective client that you just don't feel is the right fit. Maybe you said yes to a new job that feels like a huge stretch. Maybe you picked a funky new haircut or nail polish color. Maybe you turned down invites to a social gathering because you knew you needed to lay low and refill your own battery.

The list of celebrations can and should go on and on. If it makes you smile and feel proud of yourself for healthy new-to-you behaviors, it's time for you to Cheer Yourself On! Make the mental note of your celebration, jot it down in your journal, add it to a note in your phone, text a friend and share, or simply close your eyes and take a nice deep breath to let your self-pride soak into your bones!

As you integrate this Tool for Practice into your life, you will find great things will happen (and you will also recognize how many great things already *have* happened!).

Early on in your intentional Seeker-minded growth, celebrating where you are and the growth you are experiencing might not come naturally. But in time, with a dedicated, disciplined consistency, your mind will start to find things to celebrate with much more ease because you'll naturally be making YOU-Turns and evolving through countless rounds of the Growth Cycle.

It's a beautiful pattern of choosing to plant seeds and then choosing to take action to help them flourish. You are trying your little heart out to keep progressing toward the growth you want, living and learning all along the way. That's the good stuff, and it is worth celebrating. Your soul will thank you for honoring its meaningful work!

But there is one other fact that I must remind you of when it comes to the Harvest phase. This "little" detail can be a frustrating truth, but here it is: You can't rush growth. So, you'll have to learn how to let time take time.

Chapter 10
LET TIME TAKE TIME

"There is a time for everything, and a season for every activity under heaven..." Those words not only can be found in the Bible, Ecclesiastes 3:1-8, but the sentiment sings through the lyrics of The Byrds' powerful 1965 anthem, "Turn! Turn! Turn!". As the scripture and song repeat over and again, there is a time to be born and a time to die, a time to plant and a time to uproot. The very clear focus is on one powerful word—time. It makes me think of a stopwatch, pressing the button to begin the count of all the seconds that pass until pressing it again to end. Our life starts ticking the moment we breathe our first breaths and ends when we take our last. A plant's life could be measured from the day the seed is planted beneath the soil until the day its fruit is gathered or pulled from the earth. It's the cycle of life.

While that song focuses on milestone beginnings and ends of a meaningful life—as so many of us do—it's the space in between those powerful points in time that can vary wildly. And it's in those times that we can begin to stop seeing time as linear and rather as the never-ending circle and cycle that it is. While we grow, we have the opportunity to endlessly cycle through the Growth Cycle. Yet the time we spend in every phase and cycle can, should, and will vary. So, it's important that as we consider harvest, we trust that a special and unique rhythm and timing exists for every Seeker—including you. And when we trust that assertion, then we can choose to let time take time.

But how do we do that?

As I've watched JP farm over the years and as I've experienced my own growth, I see two separate and distinct yet related opportunities to help us reap more of the peace and joy that we long for as we grow: (1) embrace the seasons, and (2) have faith in the fallow. This chapter will tell you how it is normal and natural to follow the lead of Mother Nature in which there is a time to rest and a time to grow. Few trees and plants and no human can be at full bloom year-round. Regeneration and growth happens even during what appears to be rest. And so, by embracing the seasons and having faith in the fallow, you can give yourself permission to truly let time take time as you keep growing.

Embrace the Seasons

Winter, spring, summer, and fall. Those four seasons come calling in their own time and intensity wherever you might find yourself. In my part of the world, I only really experience sweltering summer and a slightly less sweltering winter. But in other parts of the world, the four seasons make themselves known and remind us of the cyclical nature of the world we live in. The moon has cycles, we women have monthly cycles, and the seasons have cycles that come and go time and time again, like the tide rolling in and out.

As you know very well from your experience, no matter where you live in the world, seasons don't hold themselves to a strict calendar or a ticking clock. One year, April can be full of snowstorms, while the next year, it feels like beach season already. We have a general idea of how things will unfold, but beyond giving each season an official date, it's impossible for anyone to truly predict *when* the seasons will change. They simply do what they do, and we can do nothing to stop or change that process. We trust that the seasons—and our bodies—will keep going on repeat. We don't sweat the small changes; we roll with them. And it should be no different as we choose to try and create our Inspired Life through conscious growth.

All Seekers must embrace the basic truth that our growth will go through seasons. Just like spring and summer days get longer, beckoning us to stay outside and lounge as the fields and yards become ready for planting. In the fall, we move into the time of shorter days, when trees shed their leaves and the air gets crisper. And then in winter, when temperatures drop, we feel called to stay in and rest. Over the 12 months of the year, our passion, intensity, focus, and determination will ebb and flow, rise and fall. We have seasons when we feel drawn to new ideas, risks, opportunities, with excitement and energy. We also have seasons when life feels slower with less fervor. But just like the seasons continue on, so does a cycle of life and growth that we must hold on to and trust.

Yet when it comes to harvest, so many of us focus on the act of reaping whatever it is we might have sown that we neglect the most powerful part of that season—it returns every year. Harvest is not a one-time wonder. It is a repeating part of the cycle of personal growth and evolution. Harvest is all too many times considered the culmination of growth rather than simply just another part of the Growth Cycle. It's not our fault that we focus on the gathering aspects of harvest. After all, we live in an achievement-oriented society that focuses on productivity. But there is another way to look at it.

Farmers know that they will have another harvest next year and the year after that. They know that it's normal to let the land rest before planting again. They look at what they did or did not accomplish in that season, the obstacles they faced, and take time to create a new plan for the next season. But the rest of us don't live in a world like that. We live in a world where we scroll through our feeds and are constantly bombarded by the highlight reels of the lives of all our "friends." Our brains constantly are looking for things to share and post so that we can show that our lives are well lived. We do not live in a world that celebrates rest.

And it's that societal training that will lead to questions like this: *What are you going to do next?*

You might have just achieved something that you were working toward or made a big transition—like leaving a relationship, changing jobs, careers, or professions, earning a new degree, or, shoot, having a kid—and someone will pop up and say, "That's great. So, what are you going to do next?"

While that question is likely not coming from a bad place, for many well-intentioned Seekers, it's daunting. It's daunting because you might not freaking know. It's a swift kick in the celebratory pants. Just when you've cycled all the way from honoring the shifting soil in your soul to a moment of breaking through and commitment to action, which led you to pacing your pursuit in the healthiest ways you could and are finally nearing an arrival of sorts as you spread stronger, deeper roots—*BOOM!* someone asks what you are going to do next. It pulls you out of the present, where you are rightly acknowledging and celebrating what you have accomplished!

The answer you might want to quickly reply with is, "Jeez,

let me relish this for a minute, why don't you?" But odds are that instead you'll smile and create some response about some plan you might have that you might or might not be terrified by. Or you'll ruminate on the fact that the closest thing to a true response is, "I have no freaking clue, buddy. Thanks for asking."

Or what if you've shared your big transition or change idea with someone, and one day out of the blue, they ask, "Why is it taking so long? You've been talking about it forever." Okay, well maybe they put it more gently than that, but you get the idea. You think, "Umm, hello, that hurts!" Hearing those words might spike your anger or frustration or trigger a crappy self-talk loop that you almost always have ready to play in your head. If this person is someone you trust and respect, though, ask them to repeat themselves slowly and elaborate. Give them a second chance because we trust these people are sharing something to help us grow. But if this is some faux friend/acquaintance who isn't in the growth game, kindly smile and push their jab to the side. You don't have to answer their questions.

Regardless of how often or when questions focused on your timeframe come up, trust that they will. And remember, these timeframe questions can even come from yourself. You might ask yourself things like: How long can this take? What is taking me so long? Why do I feel like I'm moving so slowly?

Remember that time also likes to play tricks with us. Recall the sayings that the days are long, but the years are short, or the minutes drag, but the years fly. Those crazy-sounding sayings are spot on. And it only gets worse as we get older because we have more years and moments to make our perspective of time and life seem to move at a faster and faster pace.

Growth can feel like it takes forever. Truly navigating changes for the better is like watching water boil—it seems to take forever as you stare holes through the water and pot holding it. No matter how much you obsess over it, the water won't boil faster. You just have to wait.

Time can be a soul-sucking part of the Growth Cycle. Notice I didn't say that time *is* but rather *can be* a soul-sucking part of the process. And the difference between those two perspectives comes down to truly accepting this sage advice: You don't have to suffer just because the world doesn't produce the results you want exactly when you want them.

Instead, I'm here to remind you of this: Let time take time. Here's another fact that isn't widely advertised: Faster is not always better.

Sure, speed is a good thing if you are in a timed competition, but in the game of life, each of us has a different clock that is counting down, and none of us knows when it will take its final tick. That might sound morbid, but it's true. Further, there's nothing any of us can do about it. So, rather than letting it scare us and keep us from the action that will move us closer to our Inspired Life, why not just acknowledge that the timeline for our own lives is always a mystery to us?

Allowing time to take time is an exercise of relinquishing the idea that you can control all things, or that by tightening your grip, you can somehow force your future into existence today. Hurrying anything often involves comparing your life to others or chasing other people's dreams and schedules. When you let time take time, you are hopping off the hamster wheel long enough to take true stock of your life and longings.

The things you truly, deeply love—the priceless things like your life, your courage, your confidence, your relationships, your career, your friendships, and your community—grow and develop over time. They aren't meant to be rushed. Taking life one day at a time requires patience and fortitude.

Society wants you to do everything fast. Get rich quickly! Consume as much as possible! Get lost in the 800 different types of cereal in the breakfast aisle at the grocery store! Be sure to buy those new "perfect pants" that keep popping up on your social feeds before they sell out! Advertisers and big corporations prey on our innate desire to compile and consume as well as to not be left out. And people respond in kind. We are fans of instant gratification, longing for likes to feed our validation-hungry ego. Just look at any social media account to see exactly what I am talking about.

But those things aren't real! Okay, they're real, but they're not the essence of what makes you *you*. Instead, remember that slow and steady will win your race. I will not define "slow" because that's personal and unique, but it is not unheard of for identity-shifting changes to take years to process and work through. And the sooner that you can relinquish any idea that growth should happen overnight the better. Go easy on yourself! Allow your own natural timeline to unfold.

I know it's not an easy feat because you want to change now. But trust me that allowing yourself to naturally flow through the Growth Cycle while making countless YOU-Turns will allow you to process whatever change is next in line with more calm, clarity, and peace.

It takes practice and patience to know you've made a change for the better and then choose when it's time to move on to the next growth opportunity. It takes wisdom-building exploration to discern when to let the progress take a pause or maybe even let a dream go. Again, let time take time. Embrace the seasons and trust that you know more than you think you know.

Over time, you are going to grow more and more confident in allowing your intuition to guide you. Your body might speak out and give you clues. Your loved ones might offer words that shine a light on an opportunity. You might stare out the window and daydream about what could be. You also have the Trying for Trust practice tool from Chapter 8 to use to slow down, and rest, reflect, and reaffirm your next steps.

And while you learn to embrace the seasons of your growth, you will also learn that really good things can and will happen when it might not look like it—in the offseason.

Have Faith in the Fallow

There comes a time every year when something magical happens on the farm. It's a time just after harvest is officially complete, when the last cotton bale has been wrapped and tagged. It's just after we've spent time celebrating as a family either in high fashion with a fancy meal or in a low-key way with a handmade congratulations poster made by my daughter taped to the garage door to welcome JP home.

It's the time of promise of a short respite from the hard work that had gone into the season. The fact that harvest gives way to a time where the farmer and the land can rest before it is time for a new season of growth is something we don't want to overlook. When land is left fallow—empty, without any crops in it—it is given a period of time to restore itself. Going fallow can be described as inaction or unproductivity, but it serves a valuable purpose in the spirit of growth. In fact, without that period of rest, a new Growth Cycle is impossible!

In Kate Northrup's book, *Do Less,* she outlines her belief in the power of cyclical living and describes this valuable time in our growth as the Fertile Void—a creative winter of sorts where we aren't tapped into our creative sources in the way we'd love to be. She asserts that it's in these periods that our creative energies need time to rest for new ideas and dreams to blossom and build, before they rise up and beg to be given the attention they will deserve.

That fallow ground is where we allow our hearts, souls, minds, and bodies the rest they need to restore themselves. And just like this chapter title proclaims, we have to let time take time, meaning we can't know in advance how long we might lie in fallow. We might find ourselves in holding patterns or seasons of fertile voids that appear to be halting our progress, but we have to trust that every season will eventually pass. And once we are restored, we will make a YOU-Turn and feel drawn to and pulled toward yet another Growth Cycle. Having faith in the fallow means you trust that even in rest there is growth. And even more importantly, that without rest your growth can and will suffer.

In my own life, as I neared the five-year anniversary of my first career retirement, the lyrics of the epic U2 song, "I Still Haven't Found What I'm Looking For," played on repeat in my mind as I tried to answer for myself, "What are you going to do next?"

I'd just wrapped up co-producing RON 2.0 where it felt like there was nothing but positive energy and impact to be gathered! Wendy and I had worked hard, and we took time to celebrate our personal and collective growth throughout the process. But the event came and went. The celebration was over. And I was left trying to figure out what was next for me.

I was midway through revisions with this book. Most mornings I woke up feeling blah. The excitement that I'd had as we planned and prepared and then walked on the stage to speak and share the voices of other amazing women was replaced with a dull ache of *what now?* I wrestled with that ache for a few days. Then, during one of my morning walks, I chose to walk with no music or podcast in my ears. I knew I needed to tap into my own spirit and listen to what I might need to hear. And sure enough, these words bubbled up—*you are in a holding pattern.*

To be completely honest, my reaction was: *Oh, great. Well, that sucks.* I'm pretty sure I rolled my eyes at myself and just kept putting one foot in front of the other. Holding patterns aren't my favorite—or most people's favorite. But we all have to choose to make peace with them. Something in me needed to lie fallow for a bit to rest, to restore itself, to make my heart and soul healthier for its next growth spurt.

About that time, I recalled Rebecca, a brave and wonderful woman I know who told me years earlier that she was in a funk and felt the urge to purge. She'd cleared out her home and office, but she still couldn't tell what was going on. No matter what she did, she kept feeling unsettled and stuck. But as I listened, what I shared with her was that maybe she was nesting.

Many times, women only hear about nesting during pregnancy since it's a common yet overwhelming desire to get your home ready for a new baby. Nesting is nothing more than a natural, feminine instinct to prepare for birth (and other important life phases). The urge to clean and organize, a.k.a. nest, is another way that you can have faith in the fallow. Because while those efforts appear futile (except for a really solid dose of dopamine from cleaner surroundings), it is your instincts taking over and asking you to slow down and settle in as you prepare for a growth adventure that is surely on the horizon.

We have to let time take time. And it was nearly five years after I said those words to her—*you might just be nesting, something big must be on the way*—that she was a guest on our podcast. She reminded me of my musings and said she'd never forgotten it. Then over the five years that followed, she said she grew herself and her business in ways she never saw coming. But it took time, and even though it wasn't easy, the first thing she had to do was nothing! It took her having faith in that period of nesting that including lots of rest and restoration.

So, hang tight, friend. Embrace the seasons of growth. Have faith in the fallow. And let time take time. Because when it comes to harvesting the fruits of your hard-earned growth labor, it will be worth the wait. You will look up one day and find that you are living the dream, your dream, your Inspired Life. You'll be able to celebrate yourself for the Seeker you continue to choose to be. You'll be able to celebrate every single step forward that you take. You'll be able to embrace the process and cycle of growth and not just focus on the accomplishments and achievements that are easier to define. Rather, you'll gather the bounty of a life you are proud of, where you choose to show up and try day in and day out.

But just like the years fly by, time will continue to tick by us. And to take full advantage of the life we are given, I believe that every Seeker should set aside time to set intentions for yourself. That way you are living your life on purpose with a purpose. So use this Tool for Practice as a way to choose some words of wisdom that your heart and soul know you might need to hear to keep growing!

Tool for Practice

NEW YEAR, NEW INTENTION*

*You don't need to wait for December 31 to roll around to try this Tool for Practice! But I like the name a lot, so stick with me here.

Every new year gives you the opportunity to think about resolutions, but every year, so many of us give up or just forget them. I haven't been a fan of New Year's Resolutions for years. Why? Simply because I never stuck with any of my own. They were often lofty goals that I would plan to dive in all too quickly and lose steam all too quickly, leaving me grumpy at my nonperformance. Resolutions like drinking thousands of ounces of water, journaling for 30 minutes a day, reading a new book a month, working out seven days a week, meditating first thing in the morning. Sound familiar? Honestly, I have to wonder whether that is really the best way to start off a new year.

On the other hand, intentional living matters, especially when we are allowing time to take time. Throughout all the different seasons of our growth, as we try to move closer and closer to our Inspired Life, it's important that we choose a focus and intention to guide us. A simple "I resolve to work out more this year" or "This year, I'll learn to ski" is a goal, but not a deep and personal one that will bring us closer to our Inspired Life. I only learned that lesson after far too many years, when I lived on autopilot and realized that hadn't served me well. Then in the fall of 2015, after my personal and professional worlds imploded leaving me a bit shell-shocked, I remember looking at my seemingly broken life and asking myself with a sense of despair: *How did I get here?*

I found the answer to that question in my lack of effort and attention to growth. I hadn't given myself time to dream up my Inspired Life. I hadn't consciously chosen to be a Seeker. I hadn't garnered myself to manage the growing pains I'd experience. But as I started to explore the YOU-Turns and prioritize myself and my growth journey, I decided that I needed a new plan. It was time to explore my options, and what I decided to try was to name every new year with two simple words that would embody what I wanted to grow toward and how I wanted to experience that growth.

Now, the *aha!* moment happened to coincide with a new year, but the "New Year, New Intention" exercise can be done on any day of the year. This Tool for Practice gives you the chance to get more intentional about what you want to grow toward and how you want to feel while you are living and learning!

Here's a rundown of the words I have intentionally chosen to focus on each year:

2016: Fearless Growth
2017: Balanced Freedom
2018: Calm Consistency
2019: Fun Fulfillment
2020: Explore More
2021: Faithful Focus
2022: Simple Scale
2023: Good Money

Here's the quick process you can follow to name your year or clarify your own intentions:

Step 1: Create space for quiet and curiosity. Go somewhere you can be with yourself and your thoughts, with limited to no distractions.

Step 2: Devote time to choose your words. Spend time reflecting (looking back) on what your life has been as well as time visioning (looking ahead) about what you want your life to be. Use your Seeker Statement, Dream Day, or any other Tool for Practice to get your creative juices flowing. Then use these questions as guides to help you find *two words* to honor your intention and focus:

* What do I want?

* What will I need to make that happen?

* What/how do I want to feel as I'm doing it?

Step 3: See if the words feel right. The way to do this is to say them out loud. See how they roll off your tongue and if they excite you. Have fun with it. If the words don't feel right or incite some joy or power, keep playing by going back to Step 2.

Step 4: Proclaim your words! Once you've landed on your words, find a sticky note and write them down. Then post that little note and however many more you might want all over your house, car, office—just be sure to have them somewhere you'll see them. You might even add a picture of it to your phone's lock or home screen. The key is to keep those words in front of your face. Otherwise, you risk that precious intention being out of sight, out of mind.

Then, keep those words top of mind as you live the year day by day. Each new day will have focus, awareness, and intention as you choose your next steps with your intention in mind. And what's fascinating is that every single year, I have a moment where it all comes together, and I harvest whatever wisdom I needed to learn from that year's two precious words.

I have no doubt that such awareness will happen for you too. Choose your words wisely and with a bit of whimsy, and then let time take time. At the next new year or next meaningful time for you, sit and reflect on what your words might be guiding you to-ward. Then maybe revisit Chapter 9's Tool for Practice and Cheer Yourself On again and celebrate that you've gained new insight yet again.

And that is what *Harvest* is all about: celebrating your growth and continuing to make the Seeker's ultimate choice—*Will I keep growing?*

Chapter 11

KEEP GROWING

"If you aren't growing, you're dying."

I was struck by the woman's calm and very matter-of-factness in what many would consider a very bleak observation. I was sitting with her in a room full of women at a monthly networking event. That day, I was the speaker. To begin, I had invited every woman to share what personal growth meant to them in five or fewer words. That was her response.

If you aren't growing, you're dying.

Okay, yes, that's six words, not five. But stick with me here.

To her, personal growth meant... everything. It was, in her mind, the same thing as being alive. What she meant by that statement is that at every single moment, of every single day, you have a choice to make: grow (move forward) or die (stop moving). Those six words are exactly the point that I've been trying to express to you throughout the entirety of this book. You have a massive life-changing choice to make—will you choose to grow? It's a choice that every person gets to make, and it's vital to creating and experiencing an Inspired Life.

I agree with her: If you aren't growing, you are dying. Of course, I don't mean dying in the literal sense, but if you choose *not* to keep growing, then you are choosing *not* to truly feel life flowing through your veins, and you are also choosing *not* to experience the Inspired Life that is available to you. Why would you give up all of that? If you choose not to grow, you are choosing to settle for less than you deserve.

Isn't it ironic that her words took me right back to the truth that I shared in the opening pages of this book? *A farmer dies when he stops farming.* There is something so deep in a farmer's bones and DNA that without it they simply would cease to exist. Their lifeline would be cut, their passion severed, their fervor blown out like a candle in the wind. And remember that I believe we all are born to be the farmers of our precious souls. So, if and when we ever stop planting new seeds of hope for what we want, stop tending to the choices we have along the way, stop helping ourselves grow, then we will have nothing fresh, beautiful, or new to harvest.

On that sunny afternoon, all these thoughts of dying circled back around in my mind. Of course, I wasn't ready to die—not in a literal way or in a metaphorical death of my soul. Like all the women with me that afternoon, I had a lot more growing to do. The discussion that afternoon reminded me of the choices that I made years back when my world felt like it was falling apart. I had decided that I would no longer settle. I had decided that I would not limp through life. Nope. I chose then that I would nurture my one, precious soul and learn how to be the Seeker that I knew I could be.

And you have a soul calling you to action too.

You have a soul that I believe longs to be heard. And I bet you know that now, too.

You have a soul that has hopes and dreams.

You have a soul that needs you to choose to care for and

nurture it.

You have a soul that is begging you to prioritize yourself so that you can grow together, try all the things, feel all the feelings, reap all the miraculous benefits and rewards of a life well lived.

The invitation that life presents you is clear: *Will you choose to be a Seeker?*

Remember that Seeker with a capital *S* is a person who is *attempting* to find something. There's no guarantee a Seeker will find what they are looking for, but they are choosing to try. Therefore, they are choosing to *grow* and to *live.* It all starts with *trying.*

In just a few pages you'll be done with this book, but life is going to keep "keeping on," throwing some expected and many unexpected growing pains in your way. *Will you choose to embrace change as an agent for your life-giving growth?*

You may have picked up this book originally because you had looked in the mirror and asked yourself, *"How did I get here?"* with a sense of despair and maybe even regret. I know. I've been there.

Thankfully, in 2015, I chose to finally honor my soul's longing for change. At that time, I didn't focus on regret, but nearly seven years later in my journey, just prior to writing this book, I read Daniel Pink's book, *The Power of Regret.* In my continued exploration of how to grow, I was captivated by his book and his unusual use of regret. While many focus on living life with no regrets, Pink asserts that "Regret is not dangerous or abnormal, a deviation from the steady path toward happiness. It is healthy and universal, an integral part of being human. Regret is also valuable. It clarifies. It instructs. Done right, it needn't drag us down; it can lift us up."

After I read his book (which I strongly encourage you to do as well), I realized that all those years ago when my world was falling apart, I had actually been suffering from a buildup of what he calls boldness regrets, at the heart of which Pink says is the "…thwarted possibility of growth. The failure to become the person—happier, braver, more evolved—one could have been."

For far too many years, I had been so scared to change, so scared to leave my comfort zone, so unpracticed at prioritizing myself, and so disconnected from my heart and soul, I had failed to try and become the person I believed I could be. I had not tried to accomplish new things. I had not even given myself permission to dream. Reading his book now, nearly 8 years after choosing to be a Seeker, reminded me of how far I'd come, but also gave me a renewed sense of determination.

I realized that by rethinking regret and learning how to anticipate future regrets, I had added yet another tool to my growth toolkit. I stopped to think about what I'd never want to regret when I at last neared my final days. On my deathbed, would there be anything that I dreamed of, but didn't try for, or attempt that would break my heart? If *yes*, then dang it, I would have to choose to figure out how to grow toward those things while I still had the chance.

His ideas were new to me, and they spread an even deeper root in all that I'd lived and learned on my own—that I had to not only learn how to grow, but then I'd have to choose to keep growing. And confirmed for me then after years of trying a new way of living, the math held true:

The Growth Cycle + YOU-Turns = An Inspired Life

I was able to flip the equation and realize that in order to grow forward, I had to first create a vision of what my Inspired

Life looks like. Then I could pursue the growth I wanted through the Growth Cycle armed with the YOU-Turns as a vital way to reconnect with and prioritize myself. With the powerful tool of self-reflection, I could slow myself down to see what I'd lived and learned.

Finally, with that new knowledge, I planted new seeds in my soul and cared for them as they grew, only to reap the next harvest of life lessons. I had chosen to keep growing. And if you choose to keep growing—with all the twists, turns, changing seasons, and speeds of life—you too will find the freedom to grow as you shift from a place of doubt, fear, or regret to pride, where you stop and look at your life and ask with wonder, awe, and appreciation: *"How did I get here?!"*

You have a beautiful, unique life to live. I believe in you and your dreams. But your decision will ultimately be your choice to make—will you choose to keep growing and make your Inspired Life your lived reality?

"Yes, and..."

The choice whether to grow or not will forever be yours, and I hope you choose wisely. I hope that you'll choose to try. To be the Seeker you were born to be. That you'll choose to nurture your soul. That you'll allow grace to take precedence over perfection. That you'll choose to take risks. That you won't waste the precious time you are given. That you stay true to yourself and empower others to do the same. That you will think, feel, and do hope-fueled and effort-worthy things.

Because here's the thing: The harvest isn't only about the beautiful gathering of the fruits of your labor; it's also simply the end of one cycle of growth, a closure that is necessary so that another one can begin.

But since Harvest does represent an end, albeit just a temporary one, it lends itself to some final thoughts and a final Tool for Practice. When it comes to our lives—the ones that you and I are fortunate to still be alive and kicking in right now—we know that there will come a day when our time here on Earth as we know it will be over.

We will die. I can tell you right now that my editor, Emily, kindly suggested that this observation and where I'm about to go with you is a bit bleak. She thought I should consider staying more positive, filling you with hope and inspiration as you close this book and head back to your life ready to grow.

I appreciate her feedback, but as she says, this is MY book, and the final choice is mine. So, I choose to say that I cannot and will not ignore the reality of life as we know it. We are born, we grow, and then we die. It is bleak. But it is also beautiful. It is scary. But it is also so rich and fulfilling. The good and the bad, the sweet and the sour, the highs and the lows—this is life.

Life is all about the *yes, and*. The "Yes, and.." is an exercise in being able to hold two realities at the same time, both being true, neither negating the other. Is life hard? *Yes, and* it can be so simple sometimes too. Is life full of risks? *Yes, and* those risks might lead you to the biggest rewards. Will we die? *Yes, and* we are alive right now, in this very moment.

Like every human on Earth, I had no control over the circumstances of my birth. And despite how much I'd like to know (or not, depends on the day), I have no knowledge of the details of my death. So, I choose to control what I can control. I can try to create and experience a life that I am inspired by—one that makes me feel alive, awake, and enthusiastic! In my pursuit to embrace the free will I've got to dream, and plan, and act, I know that there will be times when I will be heartbroken and hurt. But I trust there will also be times where I can barely stand the awe, wonder, and love that I feel for myself and others.

I am choosing to not fear my death, but rather to look at life as an opportunity to seize and squeeze all that I can out of each day I'm given. I want to wake up every morning and know that whatever the day holds, I can figure it out. I can live and learn and feel and deal and hurt and heal. Because I trust in the Growth Cycle and the YOU-Turns where I have found the peace, which I long for in life, resides. My life (and yours too) is not ultimately about the riches, the achievements, the long list of accomplishments... those come and go. What will last is the legacy you create in your Inspired Life. When you choose to honor the longings of your heart and soul and grow toward them, others will want to do the same. The changes you make for the better will ripple out into the world, positively impacting people you may never cross paths with.

You have the opportunity to model for your children, your family, your community, what it looks like to honor your truth—that you are meant to grow, in your own precious direction, at your own pace, toward your Inspired Life. Just like those dandelion seeds that blow off and out into the world, so will your everyday bravery, humble curiosity, and disciplined consistency. People will want to grow when they see you choosing to be the Seeker you were born and now choose to be.

So, please keep making this one important decision—to *keep growing!* Don't settle. Don't stop. Pause to pace yourself. Slow down to grow through rest, reflection, and reaffirmation of your next steps. Then—*choose to keep growing.*

Choose yourself.
Prioritize yourself.
Love yourself.
And grow, friend, grow!

But as you turn the final pages of this book, please consider giving this final Tool for Practice the time and respect it deserves. Your life and legacy are already something to be wildly proud of, but in this tool, you can practice imagining how you'd want your Inspired Life and legacy to be remembered ultimately. Take a deep breath and give yourself the time to honor your heart and soul.

Tool for Practice

CELEBRATE YOUR LIFE AND LEGACY

The unavoidable truth is that you and I will both reach a time when our life as we know it will come to an end. And while this thought can feel disconcerting to many (including me the first time I was asked to think about it), one of the most telling exercises to work through is to sit today with your beating heart thudding in perfect rhythm in the background as you write out what could one day be your eulogy.

Again, trust that I had to really push back with my editor to keep this invitation in! She worried it was too morbid, but I knew I had to include this exercise because it's a huge opportunity for you to grow. So, take a deep breath and stick with me. The word eulogy alone might conjure up not-so-pleasant feelings, but remember that you are reading this book because you want to keep growing. You want to show up as the Seeker I know you to be and make changes for the better. You might be just starting to make those changes or be knee-deep in them—either way, a powerful tool to add to your growth toolkit is to always begin with the end in mind.

What I mean is to start the journey toward as well as through growth and change with the end in mind, the vision of ultimate success and an Inspired Life. And there is no better way to get clarity on what you really want from your life than to imagine what would really matter to you in your dying days. You can think on this now and decide exactly what you'd want to be read, heard, and remembered about you and your precious life by those left behind to mourn.

Might this feel odd? *Yes.*
Is it worth the discomfort? *Yes.*
Could it be fun though? *Again, yes.*

I invite you to suspend your knee-jerk reaction to the invitation and focus on the opportunity to write a powerful and meaningful tribute to the life you've lived—and even the life you've yet to create. Focus on including whatever feels right to you. Here are ideas to prompt your reflection and writing:

* A brief overview of your life, including key milestones.

* Favorite memories or moments of honor or pride you want to be remembered.

* Favorite songs, stories, authors, quotes, or -isms that were distinctly you.

* Details about relationships with close family or friends.

* Meaningful accomplishments related to your career, hobbies, interests, and community impact.

* Moments that bring indescribable joy or laughter.

* What you longed to bring to the world.

* Nuggets of wisdom that you lived by or want to impart to others.

Write about all those things as if they had already happened. Write them out and allow yourself to feel any emotions that might present themselves. Feel the pride in the hopes you have for your life. Embrace the excitement in the dreams you have for yourself and those you love. What an honor it is to spend time dreaming of what your Inspired Life can and will become! To have pride in what you have yet to create. To know your truth that you are showing up every day willing to try and ready to grow. And to hold tight to these other truths:

Life is fragile.

Change is inevitable.

You are meant to grow *not* to settle or limp along through life.

You have options.

You have all you need to figure "it" out.

And the choices are yours to make—

Will you choose to be a Seeker?

Will you choose to dream up your Inspired Life?

Will you prepare yourself to manage the inevitable growing pains?

Will you prioritize yourself with YOU-Turns?

Will you honor shifting soil in your soul?

Will you gather the courage to act so you can break through?

Will you pace yourself as you pursue the longings of your heart?

Will you explore as a means of becoming a person firmly rooted in self-trust?

Will you embrace every Growth Cycle that comes your way?

Will you let time take time and celebrate yourself throughout it all?

Will you choose to keep growing?

My hunch is that you will. You will do all those things. You will do them in your own unique way. You will look in the mirror and see a Soul Farmer ready to get your hands dirty, as you plant, grow, and harvest your beautiful and bountiful Inspired Life!

THAT'S A WRAP

Throughout this book, I've described how nearly a decade ago I decided that I had to become a Seeker. My job wasn't satisfying anymore. I was losing touch with my marriage. Things were going off the rails, and I'm eternally grateful that in the end, I realized and changed course before it was too late. I set out on the road to find my Inspired Life. It wasn't easy. I took risks. I ramped up too fast sometimes, and I pulled back too far on other occasions. I tip-toed my way into conversations that scared me. I got a lot of things right. I also got a lot of things not-so-right. It was fun. It was meaningful. It was scary and even sad sometimes. But I learned from it all, and I grew into a woman who loves herself. It's true—I love me! And on top of that, I trust myself to nurture my soul and create my Inspired Life. I trust that not only am I ready to grow, but I trust that I can always keep growing.

I first started detailing this journey in my debut memoir, *Road to Hope.* Writing that book helped me relive parts of my life that were brutal and then heal from childhood and adult experiences that left their scars. Once it was finished, I decided the best way to celebrate the changes I was undertaking was by designing a tattoo that would serve as a daily reminder of the direction in which I needed to keep heading. Inked in the same custom font from the pages of that book, the tattoo on my right wrist carries these five important characters "ikmt."

You're probably wondering what "ikmt." stands for, as did the people who follow my Instagram page when I shared a sneak peek. There were several guesses, and one person actually got it right (way to go, Leandra). But while she might have guessed what it stood for, she couldn't possibly understand what it meant to me. For me, every time I glance down at my wrist while typing, or doing the dishes, or out for a walk on a sunny morning, I am reminded an important fact—*I know my truth.*

That tattoo was and remains special and intentional for several reasons including:

The font reminds me visually of my trek within *Road to Hope* and was my celebratory gift for making my dream become reality!

I deliberately had it put on my right wrist because the right side of the brain is believed to house creative thoughts and emotions, which fueled my writing and publishing journey.

It's in all lowercase letters to remind me to keep taking small, meaningful steps forward each and every day, knowing they'll turn into leaps of faith in their own time.

It ends with a period to remind me that while that book had an end, my journey, my growth, and my evolution continues.

And finally the message is simple. *I know my truth.* I've worked hard to find it. I'll continue to learn better and do better.

But my truth will always remain—*I am meant to grow*. I matter. My dreams matter. My relationships matter. And if I continue to choose love over fear and hope over despair, I will experience the growth, connection, and joy I long for on this earth.

ikmt.

I chose this because I wanted a permanent reminder that I must choose to keep growing. And not only that, but I am brave and bold, and I deserve to live the life of my dreams. I wanted a daily reminder that I matter—no doubt or hesitation about it. I know my truth, and knowing that truth is an ultimate act of self-love and devotion that I will cling to. I must continue to allow my truth to grow and evolve, and that's just what I'll do.

But it's not easy. That's why nearly every single morning I repeat these words as a way to feed my soul:

I am brave.
I have bold dreams.
I am full of confidence and conviction.
And I will continue to grow day in and day out—
Not only because I am capable,
But because I know that I deserve all that life has to offer me.

Please use those words to breathe light and life into your own heart and soul as you keep growing. My wish for you is that you give yourself the time and attention you deserve to discover your very own truth. But trust that my truth is also true for you—*you are meant to grow!*

My Parting Words of Gratitude

Before you venture off into the life of your choosing, allow me share my most sincere gratitude and excitement that you joined me on the pages of this book. Thank you for coming. Thank you for reading page after page of what I hope sparks your soul with curiosity and fills your heart with hope.

Thank you for loving yourself enough to learn more about how you can grow into the confident, determined, truth-seeking creature you are. My heart bursts thinking of all that you are capable of living and learning now that you can see the math by which to create your Inspired Life.

The Growth Cycle + YOU-Turns = An Inspired Life

But enough talk. It's time for you to get out there and do what Soul Farmers do—sow precious seeds of change to reap your most incredible Inspired Life!

ACKNOWLEDGMENTS

As a mother of two, I know what it takes to birth a baby. And let me tell you, after writing my first book, I decided that writing and publishing a book is much the same. That's why it is my honor to take the time to celebrate all the people who helped me nurture and bring this second book-baby of mine to life in the world.

Ally, thank you for being the exact right person to help me prepare to publish in such an authentic and organized way. You welcomed me into your home in Nashville where we let the ideas flow out and onto notecards. The curious and creative process you walked me through was a gift. Walking out with a sandwich baggie that held my heart scribbled on over a hundred notecards was such a fun first step in creating this book.

Book Launchers' team, thank you for being talented and able guides through the self-publishing journey. A special thanks to Dan, who had the courage to read the first draft of the manuscript and decide that it needed help. Your suggestion that I work with a coach to make the material more meaningful was a hit to my ego, but after a quick pity-party, I knew you were right. Giving me the opportunity to practice the humility I write about was a gift (even if I didn't enjoy receiving it initially).

Emily, you came in to coach me and my manuscript toward better versions of ourselves, and you did it. You were patient and kind as you helped me find my own path forward. You challenged me to reimagine what this book could look like and unknowingly led me to another personal Growth Cycle. Knowing I had you in my creative corner was a gift that I'll forever be thankful for.

A special thank you to the women who have trusted me as a coach. It has been a true honor and gift to help you all find your way toward your Inspired Lives. Also, I appreciate every woman who has supported and attended *Ready or Not* (RON and RON 2.0) events and listened to the *You Just Don't Know It Yet* podcast. The community of strong-willed women that we're building gives me such hope and I'm thankful.

I must also thank friends who supported me from day one. Alisa and Kim got the love they deserve in the pages of the book, but allow me to thank a few others here as well.

Janine, thank you for being a strong yet silent type who always lets me know you believe in me and my work. And thank you for having the most peaceful studio/she-shed that served as my writing oasis on many a day. This book wouldn't be here without you or your Zen haven.

Wendy, I had been longing for a partner in my work, and you seamlessly came into my life ready to make things happen. I feel stronger when I am around you, ready for challenges I didn't even know I wanted to conquer. Thank you for shamelessly plugging my first book on the podcast every week, and for celebrating me every baby step of the way on this one.

Nicole, knowing that I have a friend that I can be real with is such a gift. And even when I felt like I was repeating my book-writing woes over and over at our meetups, you repeatedly let me know that you believed I had something to say, something that mattered, and your affirmations mattered so much to me.

Kylie, from our reconnection back in COVID days, I've felt fiercely supported by you. We've both grown since those Calls for Gratitude, and I'm proud of us both. Thank you for being the ever-reliable woman, mother, friend, and command central that I could count on as I worked my way through life and this book.

Taylor and Chelsea, you two quickly proved that magic happens when women come together as cheerleaders, collaborators, and graceful challengers. You two have dreams that inspire me to keep growing. And I can't thank you two enough for helping me nail down the title and subtitle of this book as we brunched over omelets and migas. Goosebumps and tears of joy were shared and the truth that women are better together was seared into my Seeker heart.

Rachel, you came into my life when I needed help. You were kind and gracious as you ushered me through a season of growth. Thank you for being the farmer-in-training that you are so you can get corny with me and bring fun to the work I'm trying to bring to the world.

Peyton and Peggy, thank you both for being strong-willed women who show up ready to grow and inspire me to do the same.

And to Lindsey, last but certainly not least. Who knew that when we met nearly a decade ago, we'd work together to usher our book babies into the world. You said Yes! when I asked you to create a song that would embody all Soul Farmer was about. And I could not be prouder of what we created together. I will be forever thankful for your obsessive creativity, irreverent humor, and the safe, trusted place you hold in my heart.

Then to my family who mean so much to me and deserve a shout-out. So, drumroll please for Sid, Shirley, Mandy, Richard, Parker, Mallory, Jimmy, Peggy, Blake, Kristen, Tyler Bree, Riley, Blakely, Bennett, Lindsey, Brad, Archer, and Dylan.

And to Marilyn and Gary, thank you for loving me as I do my best to honor JoAnn. Her life will forever have meaning and value as it inspires me to honor every moment I have and trust myself to keep growing.

And a few specific notes of thanks to:

Kristen, thank you for your marathon Marco Polo messages, for consistently asking how things were going, and bolstering my confidence as I made progress. Time and time again, you helped me feel more at peace throughout the process, and I'm so grateful for that.

Mandy, may we always bond over tattoos and sarcasm. I always know you have my back and that you'll speak to me through the perfectly timed meme, bringing a smile to my face when life really isn't "fine." Having you as my sister, knowing you will always be there with nonjudgmental, unconditional love for me and this book has been and will forever be a game changer.

To my parents, Shirley and Sid, and my in-laws who I'm lucky to have as my second set of parents, Peggy and Jimmy, thank you all for supporting me through yet another creative venture and for always showing up to love and care for me, JP, and our kiddos. Knowing that I have you all in our corner is a gift that I pray you know I don't take for granted.

To my children, Trace and Elizabeth, I love you both and can't express how much joy you bring to my life. Without knowing it, you both give me the inspiration I need to trust my gut and pursue my own potential, because one day I want you both to trust yourselves and do the same—go and make your dreams your reality! I believe both of you can do anything you set your mind to, and I can't wait to see how your Inspired Lives grow and evolve over time!

JP, my high school sweetheart and husband, I am so proud of how far we've come in our own growth journeys, but also what we've worked to create together. Thank you for sharing your farmer soul with me and helping me reimagine this book. To have *Soul Farmer* forever linked to you and your passion for agriculture makes me smile, and I pray makes you proud. Proud of who you are, all you have to offer, and how our dreams can come together to make something really special.

And finally, to God (or at least who I understand God to be). Thank you for being something bigger than I'll ever be able to fathom, but also small enough to feel close to in quiet moments. For giving me nature and moments of woo-woo that leave me in awe, unable to understand how it all works, yet feel completely connected to a truth. For sending deer to cross my path and repeating numbers on the clock just to let me know you're thinking about me. Life is a freaking mystery and I'm here for it, so thank you for giving me a curious and faithful soul. And for giving me a soul that longs to love. Because I pray that in the end, this book, this life, my life will be one that is remembered for that simple, single life-giving force: love. ♥

THANK YOU FOR COMING!

hope *Soul Farmer* inspired you toward the growth you deserve! To continue following me on my own journey, check out the fun at denajansen.com. Hope to see you there!

Printed in the USA
CPSIA information can be obtained
at www.ICGtesting.com
LVHW040526020224
770666LV00002BA/9